CLOSING THE GAP

The Trial of
Trooper Robert Higbee

By D. William Subin

COMTEQ
PUBLISHING™
MARGATE, NEW JERSEY

Margate, New Jersey

A division of ComteQ Communications, LLC

www.ComteQpublishing.com

Printed in the United States
10 9 8 7 6 5 4 3 2 1

ISBN 978-1-935232-69-8

ComteQ Publishing
101 N. Washington Ave. • Suite 1B
Margate, New Jersey 08402
609-487-9000 • Fax 609-487-9099
Email: publisher@ComteQpublishing.com

Book & cover design by Rob Huberman

To all law enforcement and emergency responders whose split-second decision-making stays with them the rest of their lives.

Acknowledgements

To my wife Petie, and my sons Jeremy, Daniel and Zachary, and my brother Dave and sister-in-law Elissa, for their support during the trial.

To the faith of my client Robert Higbee and his wife Beth and their families.

To the hundreds of STFA members led by David Jones and Chris Burgos.

To the hundreds of present and retired law enforcement personnel, attorneys, experts, and even former judges, across the country, who volunteered their time to help us, particularly Barry Wythe, John Heenan, John Campbell and Lou Horvath.

To my trial team, including Investigator Manny Ridgeway and Attorney Donna Lee Vitale.

To my faithful office staff of Veronica Rivera, office manager and Dot Hand, secretary.

To readers Pat Goldstein and Barbara and Jennifer Altman, Jessie Noa, Esq. and Roger Adelman, Esq.

To my dedicated and unselfish copyright Attorney Joe Youngblood III.

To Illustrator Carl L. Rosner, Editor Mike Valentino, and Publisher Rob Huberman. Thank you.

Table of Contents

Author's Preface

There are several reasons why I chose to write this book and why I deemed the trial in this case to be the most excruciating and challenging in approximately forty-two years of practicing law at the time.

First, this case was significant to law enforcement agencies across the country. Concerns were expressed that if a conviction resulted and Robert Higbee's actions were deemed criminal, the adverse effect on police, emergency responders, ambulance drivers, and firefighters could be immense. Imagine if the courageous individuals who respond to any emergency in order to protect us, began to second-guess themselves and hesitate to take action for fear that an unintentional mistake might lead to criminal charges and prison.

Secondly, throughout the time I was defending Trooper Higbee, I was concerned that, as his legal counsel, I would somehow fail him. As an experienced criminal attorney I was convinced, as a matter of law and on the merits of the case, that Robert was innocent of any criminal wrongdoing. It was up to me to present the facts, and to see to it that he was acquitted.

Throughout these proceedings, Robert's conduct convinced me of his strength of character. This only added to the excruciating stress I felt every day, knowing I must do my best to defend what I had come to recognize as a fine man.

D.W.S. 7/1/13

Introduction

Thirty-four-year-old New Jersey State Trooper Robert Higbee lay on his back in an Atlantic City Hospital room. His 6'8" frame hardly fit into the bed. Just hours before at 10:00 p.m., Higbee sustained a concussion when the patrol car in which he was "closing the gap" on a speeder, collided with a van crossing through an intersection ahead of him. Tragically, the two teenage sisters in the van died at the scene.

The next morning, I received a phone call from the State Troopers Fraternal Association of New Jersey (STFA), the organization that represents the state's law enforcement officers. I was already on their approved attorney's list and had previously answered "critical incident matters" on their behalf. I was now being asked to represent Trooper Higbee regarding any repercussions related to the accident.

Within an hour I was at the hospital. Higbee was still in a daze. I had no idea at that moment I met him, how closely our lives would become connected.

Five months later, a Cape May County grand jury indicted Trooper Higbee on the charge of vehicular homicide, a crime that carries a penalty of up to twenty years in prison. My job was to establish conclusively that Higbee had acted neither intentionally nor recklessly, only that he had made a tragic mistake in the dark of night, at a poorly marked intersection in rural Cape May County, New Jersey.

The heaviest burden that can be placed upon a defense attorney is in knowing that the fate of an innocent person rests in your hands. The following two-and-a-half years would prove to be the most demanding and excruciating I have ever experienced in my career as a criminal trial lawyer.

Chapter 1

Lives are intertwined by unforeseen events...

The tragedy took place around 10:00 p.m. September 27, 2006 at a poorly lit and badly marked intersection in rural Cape May County, New Jersey.

An outstretched piece of land jutting south from the rest of New Jersey, the county is a unique combination of summertime seasonal resorts, small towns, rural farmland and woods. The locals travel back roads from Memorial Day through Labor Day to avoid the congestion on the Garden State Parkway, a toll road bisecting the peninsula from north to south ending just before Victorian Cape May.

Marmora, a part of Upper Township, is so small there is no local police force. Children in Upper Township attend the Ocean City High School a few miles to the east. There are pockets of mini shopping malls along Route 9, the busy road that parallels the Garden State Parkway, along with some 24-hour convenience stores, gas stations, and pizza parlors open at night. Driving south on Route 9, you intersect a two-lane road called Old Tuckahoe Road (County Road 631). Turning right, some distance later, that road intersects a smaller road named Stagecoach Road (County Road 667), running roughly north and south and parallel to Route 9.

Stagecoach Road is about 100 years old. It may have been a dirt road before the county paved it. Tourists or those unfamiliar with the area would probably never venture from Route 9 west to this intersection of Tuckahoe and Stagecoach.

5

Locals avoid the traffic on Route 9 and the Garden State Parkway as much as possible to do their errands. They, however, might be familiar with a little group of stores called Wayside Village along Tuckahoe Road. They might go to the little restaurant or the ice cream stand there during the day. But at night there is little or no activity in this largely residential and rural area. Probably the only store open in the evening hours is the Wawa convenience store on Route 9.

There are no full time firefighters or rescue squads in this area, only volunteers, and like in many other areas outside New Jersey cities, law enforcement is provided by the New Jersey State Police. Unlike local police, New Jersey State Police troopers are assigned to this area from the Woodbine Barracks, typically spend some months in the roughly 40-square-mile area, and then move on to other assignments in the state.

The local residents typically escape the massive crowds and excitement of the seaside resorts to the east. But one event changed all that.

Seventeen-year-old Jacqueline Becker was close to her nineteen-year-old sister Christina. Five-foot-eight with dark brown wavy hair, Jacqueline was a senior at Ocean City High School and loved history, art and drama. She spoke Italian and Spanish and loved languages with a base in Latin. Her outgoing personality was perfect for school plays.

With lighter brown wavy hair, older sister Christina wore glasses, was heavyset, and was more reserved. She had graduated a few years earlier from Ocean City High School and now attended neraby Richard Stockton College of New Jersey. Her dream was to own a bed and breakfast with her mother, Maria Caiafa, so she was taking culinary courses to further her career plans. Christina was working her way through college delivering medicine to seniors as part of her duties at an Ocean City pharmacy.

Both girls were gentle and loving. Both had baby-sat for neighbors in the Upper Township area while staying with their maternal grandparents Caesar and Geraldine Caiafa, which they did often. Maria has been the long-time principal at a middle school in Northfield, a larger community in Atlantic County. Maria's parents loved to have Christina and Jacqueline at their home in Upper Township. All five were often together. Grandfather Caesar talked about them as "his girls," describing Jacqueline as his "white rose" and Christina as "red rose," a reference to their complexions.

* * *

Seventeen-year-old Josh Wigglesworth attended Ocean City High School. Also a senior, he lived with his mother and stepfather in Upper Township. Like many teens his age, he enjoyed being able to drive his own car, a 1994 black BMW. Slight of build and slender, he does not stand out in a crowd. His demeanor is mild and not aggressive or assertive. He worked in the family tile business when not in school. He had a girlfriend who lived not far away on a side street just off of Stagecoach Road, about a mile south of the Wayside Village intersection. So as not to worry his parents, Josh was aware of the rules at home about coming home too late after visiting his girlfriend, especially on school nights.

* * *

Thirty-four-year-old New Jersey State Trooper Robert Higbee is an imposing six-foot-eight and weighs close to 250 pounds. His friends and former coaches refer to him as the "gentle giant." Robert grew up in Atlantic County to the north, and played basketball and football for Ocean City High School's rival, Mainland High School, winning awards and gaining recognition for his prowess on the football field. He also played football in college, first at University of Virginia and then transferring to the "Blue Hens" of the University of Delaware, closer to home. Robert tried out for the Dallas Cowboys but was cut from the training camp in Texas because they needed another position filled at the time of his tryout. Robert also did a short professional basketball stint around the country and in Europe, touring with the team opposing the Harlem Globetrotters. By the time he settled back down in the Somers Point area in Atlantic County, Robert Higbee was married to Bethany and had embarked on a career with the state police.

Robert went through extensive training at the rigorous state police academy at Sea Girt, New Jersey. In both physical and mental
terms, that training has been compared with the best in the country,
like the FBI training at Quantico, Virginia, where only the strongest
and best emerge as law enforcement officers. As a "road trooper"
for about five years before that night, Robert had patrolled the su-
perhighways of the Garden State, handling various traffic and criminal violators. He had no blots on his service record and no
disciplinary actions of any kind. Careful and meticulous, according
to his superiors' evaluations, he was given the additional assignment
of coaching newer troopers, when he was assigned to the Woodbine
Barracks about seven months earlier. Robert helped his young
trainees gain patrol experience by concentrating on the higher-crime
areas within his jurisdiction.

Unlike some of the other troopers in the barracks, Robert Higbee
was only somewhat familiar with the intersection of Tuckahoe and
Stagecoach Roads, having had no reason to pass by there except for
a few times he may have been on patrol during daylight hours. The
troopers from the Woodbine barracks patrol a large regional area,
much of it rural with narrow back roads, residential developments
and some commercial and tourist areas that account for the bulk of
their arrests for traffic and criminal activities.

The territory Robert covered was so expansive that he had to
keep maps in his patrol car or to sometimes ask the dispatcher for
directions in order to locate an address within the area where state
troopers like himself provided the only police presence. Becoming
familiar with every turn and intersection was just not practical.

Trooper Higbee also did not know what many locals believed—
*that the intersection of Old Tuckahoe and Stagecoach Roads at night
could be perilous.*

* * *

The close-knit Italian family of three generations gathered for
dinner at an Ocean City restaurant. The girls wanted to leave early,
and they asked their grandfather if they could borrow his Dodge
van to go back to the grandparents' house, where the girls were stay-

ing. It was only a short ride from the restaurant. Upon arriving they found they needed milk for breakfast, and decided to drive to a local store on Route 9.

Christine was in the passenger's seat and Jacqueline was in the driver's seat, even though she had only a learner's permit, and Christine was two years shy of the New Jersey age requirement to supervise Jacqueline's driving at night. For some unknown reason, Christine Becker did not put on her seat belt. They turned right, off of Route 9 and onto Tuckahoe Road where the posted speed limit is 35 miles per hour.

Suddenly, as they approached the intersection of Stagecoach Road, there was a tremendous crash. Then there was darkness and silence.

* * *

Seventeen-year-old Josh Wigglesworth had been at his girlfriend's house that evening. When he realized he was past his 10:00 p.m. curfew, he sped off down the road, hoping to make it home before he was noticed missing by his parents. His foot hit the accelerator as he headed north. For a brief time he was on the road alone, when suddenly he saw a pair of headlights heading in his direction in the opposite lane. As he passed the oncoming vehicle, he realized it was a New Jersey State Police patrol car.

Josh quickly glanced at his dashboard and believed his headlights were not on, only the fog lamps of the BMW in which he was driving. He flipped on his headlights and began to slow down.

Josh watched in his rear view mirror as the patrol car turned around and began to follow him. He had a lead on the police of at least 0.2 miles. He then lost sight of the trooper's headlights for a few seconds as he reached a slight elevation in the road. As Josh came down off the rise, he passed the Frito Lay warehouse on his right and the car wash on his left. He continued driving.

Crossing the intersection, he saw no red lights and heard no siren behind him, so he figured that there was no reason to stop. Josh had been through the drill before...the red lights come on and a siren sounds until the cop got close enough to run his license plate.

As Josh made it to the next intersection at Roosevelt Road, his headlights illuminated the red stop sign. He then heard a noise from behind him that sounded like a crash. As he looked into his rear view mirror he saw bright lights at the intersection of Tuckahoe and Stagecoach. He thought he also heard the sound of a horn blaring.

Josh Wigglesworth turned right onto Roosevelt and went directly home. As he pulled up to his house he heard the sound of the volunteer fire and rescue horn blaring its signal for help. He ran into his house to reassure his mother that he was all right. Josh hoped she would not notice the time. He said nothing to her about the accident he had just seen

* * *

Rob Higbee has a routine. Even though his wife Beth goes to sleep early so she can be at her job in the morning, Robert stays up until around 1:00 a.m. He sleeps until 11:00 a.m. so that he will be wide awake for his night shift. He drinks no alcohol and takes no medicine that would impair him from being alert.

On September 27, 2006, Robert did some chores around the house. He showered and changed after jogging around the neighborhood. He was in his slate blue uniform, checking the computer information at the barracks in preparation for his 6:00 p.m. to 6:00 a.m. shift. This time, there were no warrants to be served or suspects reported to be out on the streets. Cape May County was in no way immune from robberies, drug deals, or homicides. Troopers have often been faced with armed motorists in various standoffs.

Every day on patrol was different. Throughout the summer, Robert took his cadet trainee to areas where the cadet might have more opportunities to make arrests. The cadet was off that night, so Robert decided to patrol some areas in which he was less familiar. Robert checked out his assigned 2005 Ford Crown Victoria patrol car to be sure all of his equipment was working and headed out on patrol. He made some stops during the course of his shift, issuing warnings instead of tickets to drivers with headlights out and other minor infractions. As part of his duties, he would check the locks and doors of local businesses along Route 9.

Robert stopped to escort the owner/instructor of a dance studio to her car in a poorly lit parking lot after her students had left. Robert then drove north passing the Triton Tavern. No activity tonight, so he moved on. He traveled Old Tuckahoe Road, up along the deserted highways through woods, undeveloped land and some swamp areas.

The trooper headed further north toward the more developed spots in Upper Township. He had been around the area of Wayside Village during the daylight hours when the restaurants were open. But now, just before 10:00 p.m., everything was closed, so he turned right on Stagecoach Road just before he got to Route 9, and headed south through some of the residential neighborhoods heading back toward areas that might yield more activity.

Suddenly, he observed a pair of oncoming headlights approaching rapidly in his direction on the opposite side of the road. He could not immediately see the driver or details of the car. His radar activated a warning that told him the oncoming vehicle was going 65 mph, almost twice the speed limit for that stretch of road. As he locked in the radar signal, Robert pulled off the road. He checked for traffic and made a "K-turn" to head back in the opposite direction, since his patrol car could not negotiate the narrow highway to complete a U-turn.

Robert was not able to make out the license plate on the fast moving vehicle. He could only tell that it was dark-colored, but he could not yet call it in to dispatch. The only things he could see in the distance were two circular taillights. Robert fixed his eyes on the target and attempted to close the gap with the speeding vehicle. His training and state police protocol took over—no red lights and siren until he could get close enough to call in a description and license plate to dispatch. He could not yet pull over the suspect. Robert needed to find a safe spot off the road that would not pose a danger to passing motorists. He could not let the suspect dart away down a side street, and he still needed to get close enough to read the license plate.

Robert reached out to grab the radio's microphone, checked the radar and looked all around. He watched for other traffic, obstacles in the road and for signs the suspect might be trying to flee. The taillights of the car ahead flickered for a few seconds. He then lost sight of the car. As he saw the car again, he was vaguely aware that he had just passed a Stop Ahead sign somewhere in the darkness on the right hand side of the road. Robert knew he would need to slow down, activate his overhead red flashing lights, and look both ways for oncoming cars at the intersection when he got to the stop sign. But where exactly the stop sign was ahead, he wasn't sure.

Then the suspect's headlights illuminated a stop sign just ahead of the speeding car. Robert immediately focused his attention on the speeder's taillights and closed the gap on the speeder. Suddenly, there was a flash of light. Robert slammed on his brakes. There was a tremendous crash and then there was only darkness and silence.

* * *

Anthony Cinaglia used to be a tough union organizer. At 47 years old he was now a consultant, trying to put his life together. He used to have a relationship with Melinda Lipstein and he was trying to help her talk about some things in her life. They would just sit and talk, like old times. Maybe get some ice cream, but the little stand at Wayside Village was closed for the night.

Melinda sat on the railroad tie in the parking lot, with her back to Old Tuckahoe Road, facing Anthony and the closed Wayside stores. He paced back and forth looking at her sitting under the tree. Her face was barely visible to him in the dim light from the store windows behind him. An occasional passing car was the only sound in the background as they carried on their conversation. Anthony thought he heard the sound of a car coming from around the corner of the building to his left. By the time he looked in that direction down the road toward Stagecoach, something had happened.

Melinda did not see anything behind her back and to her right as she sat looking at Anthony. Then she heard a crash from the darkened intersection. Anthony rushed toward the sound, then ran back to get Melinda's cell phone to call 911. The garbled message through the regional communications dispatcher in Ocean City was about an accident on Tuckahoe near Route 9 in Upper Township.

* * *

Seventeen-year-old Michael Taylor had to ride with his father while his car was in the shop. His fifty-seven-year-old father, Robert had driven Michael in Robert's Mazda to pick up a CD Michael had inadvertantly left in his car at the shop. They were on their way home from their errand when they turned down St. Martin's Place and then made a left heading south on Stagecoach Road.

It was dark on the stretch of road above Tuckahoe, surrounded on both sides by dense woods. Nothing unusual caught the attention of father and son until their headlights illuminated an animal scurrying across the road in front of them and into the bushes on the side on the road. They figured their headlights had startled maybe a possum or a muskrat.

The dense trees and underbrush on the sides of Stagecoach Road obscured Robert Taylor's view of the upcoming intersection at Tuckahoe. You can't see what is coming from either direction until you creep out into Tuckahoe to look both ways. Robert Taylor had barely glanced to his right when he heard a car approaching rapidly. He never saw the white van hit them. There was a crash. The impact sent shattered glass from his driver's side window flying onto Robert as they sat at the stop sign. He felt blood on his face.

Michael did not see the white van either. He heard the sound of a car he thought was accelerating and saw headlights coming in their direction right before the crash. In an instant there was impact on the driver's side as Michael sat frozen in the passenger's seat. Then he saw a trooper patrol car come to an abrupt stop in the trees to his right, careening over the curb into the bushes.

* * *

Janet Harmelin was a registered nurse for some twenty years before she retired to take over as office manager for her husband's medical practice. They lived a few miles south of Tuckahoe on Stagecoach Road. She was coming back home on the main road from Ocean City on Roosevelt Boulevard and turned left, heading down Stagecoach toward Tuckahoe. She was vaguely aware on her left of a white van off to the side of the road. As she got closer to the intersection at Tuckahoe she saw two more vehicles that appeared damaged. One was right in front of her at the stop sign; another was in the woods to her right. She quickly got out of her car, relying upon her training and experience to make some quick assessments, because no emergency crews were there yet.

She was about to call 911 when a male voice indicated he had just done that. She checked the Mazda. Michael Taylor recognized her and asked, "Mrs. Harmelin, what are you doing here?" Janet quickly determined neither he nor his father had life-threatening injuries. She turned her attention to the mangled patrol car against the trees in the brushes to her right. The state trooper was still in the driver's seat. He kept moving his arm toward his chin and up and down toward his chest as if he was trying to reach for a radio. He was not alert and Janet could get no verbal response from him, but he appeared to be breathing. She started back down the road to check on the van, but saw emergency vehicles arriving.

Janet now returned her attention to the trooper who was lying across the seat on his back, trying to get up. She tried to have him stay there, as she saw Chief Jay Newman of the Marmora volunteer Fire and Rescue squad approaching.

* * *

Chief Jay Newman is one of those small town individuals who dedicates a good deal of his spare time to public service. He is stocky, middle aged and balding, but with a robust appearance. He is a funeral director, but he is best known as an elected representative on the Upper Township governing body, as well as for his long-time work as head of the volunteer firefighter and rescue squad. Chief Newman took numerous courses for EMT and firefighter training. He is actively involved in the regional Chiefs Association. He makes himself available on short notice by radio or phone dispatch to respond to emergencies in his hometown.

That night, Chief Newman was at his home adjacent to his business on Route 9 a short distance south of the intersection with Tuckahoe Road in Marmora. He received the alert from Ocean City Dispatch at 10:01 p.m. to respond to a serious accident at Route 9 and Tuckahoe. He immediately responded by driving north on Route 9 but could see no accident when he arrived there. He thought to himself that the location had to be at Tuckahoe and Stagecoach Roads, where there had been some twenty-six previous accidents in the past few years. As part of his elected duties on the Upper Township Committee, Chief Newman had been instrumental in sending some strong resolutions to the County of Cape May, urgently requesting a traffic control device be installed at the Stagecoach and Tuckahoe Roads intersection. Both being county roads, preliminary approval for changes came from the county, not from the township. He thought to himself that this accident had to be at Stagecoach as well. So he turned his emergency vehicle, with blue lights flashing, and headed down toward Stagecoach. Chief Newman reported in to dispatch that he arrived at the actual accident scene at 10:06, within about five minutes of the original dispatch call.

Chief Newman saw the state police patrol car off the roadway in the trees with one occupant still in the vehicle. The Mazda minivan was stopped just east in the roadway at the same corner, about twenty-five feet from the patrol car. The minivan contained two occupants. He saw a third vehicle, a Dodge minivan, with two female occupants, about one hundred fifty feet north of the intersection and partially off of the roadway to his right. He jumped out of his truck and went over to the collapsed police car in the trees, since it was nearest to him. The trooper inside was sprawled across the front seat with his head toward the passenger's seat. Jay checked for and found no life- threatening injuries, and then looked to the Mazda. There was damage from the front tire to the rear bumper on the driver's side. The driver appeared to be pinned inside the vehicle and was bleeding from his face. He was semi-coherent but without life-threatening injuries.

The passenger, a younger man, was already out of the car and did not appear to be hurt. Chief Newman quickly looked up the road toward the Dodge minivan and requested a trauma helicopter be dispatched, due to the severity of the accident. He rushed up to the minivan, seeing both arms of the one girl and one arm of the other were hanging outside of the driver's side window. One girl was on top of the other. Chief Newman saw massive amounts of blood and head trauma to both individuals. He got no response to his shouts and found neither to be breathing. Other emergency rescue crews, state police, firefighters, and ambulances began to arrive to treat the victims. Chief Newman turned his attention to extricating the driver of the Mazda from his vehicle and to see that the trooper was transported by ambulance. Unfortunately, he could do nothing further for the two young girls in the Dodge minivan.

Chapter 2

Within five minutes of the accident it was known that a state trooper was involved, so notifications went out to the Woodbine Barracks immediately for additional response. Soon afterwards, the station commander was notified, and additional troopers and supervisors were sent to the scene. Among those who arrived quickly to the intersection was Trooper John Schulke, who lived in the area and was more familiar with that place than most of his fellow officers. The first report he received was that the accident took place at Roosevelt and Stagecoach, but Schulke knew from previous accidents that the location was probably the one with the stop sign off to the right at Wayside Village at Tuckahoe. The shift supervisor, Sgt. Anthony Mertis, arrived at the scene in a patrol car driven by Trooper Saul. By the time they arrived, fire personnel had lit up the area with high intensity lighting and other troopers and rescue trucks had blocked off traffic.

Within eight minutes of the first 911 call, a request had gone out for critical response from EMT as well as for medevac helicopter units, because it appeared there were possibly three critical victims from the crash. The emergency medical responders at the scene examining Christina and Jacqueline Becker were, however, unable to detect any signs of life. At 10:32 p.m., by means of telemetry transmitted by them to a doctor at the regional trauma center, the girls were officially pronounced dead at the scene.

Because of the fatalities, a major investigation was immediately begun, even before the remaining victims were taken to the hospital.

Trooper Schulke had to assist Trooper Higbee, who had tried to leave his vehicle intending to aid the others. Higbee had just struggled to get out of his car when Schulke arrived on the scene.

At first Higbee attempted to walk up the road to check on the others. But then he had to grab unsteadily on to Schulke to keep from falling. Schulke thought Higbee was only semi-conscious. and saw to it that Higbee was transported with EMTs by ambulance to the Atlantic City Medical Center, the nearest major trauma unit. Notification was sent out to Sergeant John McMahon in charge of the state police Fatal Accident Unit South, and to Lt. Eugene Taylor of the Cape May County Prosecutor's Office.

* * *

Sgt. John McMahon had worked his way up through the ranks of the state police, gathering training, experience, and expertise in investigation of accidents. He was certified as an accident reconstructionist, recognized through education and testing as an expert in figuring out how and why accidents happen. In more than a decade of state police work, he had spent a number of years focusing on the causes of fatal accidents. He had been involved in over 800 previous fatals. He now headed the investigative arm of the state police for all fatal accidents in the southern half of New Jersey. His reports and testimony were utilized and recognized for their excellence by county prosecutors, insurance companies, and the New Jersey Department of Transportation.

McMahon and his staff needed to carefully measure and record every observable detail of the scene of the three car accident to determine how it happened, who may have been at fault, and to come to conclusions that might prevent future fatalities. Upon his arrival he was acutely aware that he must be thorough and objective, knowing that his report would be carefully scrutinized by various agencies, particularly because a New Jersey state trooper had been involved in the accident. He knew the prosecutor of Cape May County would independently review his findings. Oversight would also take place by his superiors in the state police and perhaps the attorney general of the state.

At the scene McMahon met with the shift supervisor, Sgt. Anthony Mertis, who directed him to the white 2002 Dodge Caravan minivan. The vehicle had sustained heavy damage to the left front corner. The left front door and wheel assembly were crushed and the wheel was folded under the vehicle. The body of one victim was covered by a sheet on the northbound lane of Stagecoach having been removed by emergency responders. The second deceased was still inside the vehicle. Turning south he observed a white Mazda mini van at its final rest on the shoulder of the northwest corner of the intersection. That vehicle had moderate damage to the left side and front end.

McMahon detected a clump of long, dark colored hair wedged behind the leading edge of the driver's door of the Mazda, along with two blood trails approximately ten inches apart extending down the length of the vehicle's left side. The top trail was below the level of the windows and the second was across the middle of the doors. McMahon was advised that the driver and passenger of the Mazda, Mr. Taylor and his son Michael, had been transported to Shore Memorial Hospital in Somers Point to be treated for injuries.

He then observed the 2005 white Ford Crown Victoria with state police insignia on its side door, at the northwest corner of the intersection, west of the Mazda. The patrol car had heavy damage to its right front corner where it was stopped against a tree. The left side of the vehicle was against a large tree stump. McMahon and his colleagues then took careful measurements, looking for debris, skid marks, fluids that may have spilled, and other evidence to try to recreate the dynamics of the accident.

Very preliminary conclusions could be drawn that night. The trooper's car going north on Stagecoach apparently had not completely stopped at the stop sign at Tuckahoe, and his right front struck the left driver's front of the Dodge van going west on Tuckahoe, which had the right of way. Both vehicles then collided with the Mazda, which was stopped in the northwest corner of the intersection southbound on Stagecoach and the patrol car came to rest in the trees. The Dodge van scraped along the side of the Mazda and came to rest approximately 130 feet further north of the intersection on the shoulder of Stagecoach Road. After examination of the victims and the interior of the Dodge van it would appear that the passenger was not restrained by a seat belt, and was thrown to her left by the impact, striking the driver. Both were partially ejected through the driver's side window. They sustained massive head injuries by striking their heads along the side of the Mazda. Those injuries alone would seem to have been fatal, but an autopsy by the medical examiner would have to make that determination.

Sgt. McMahon was familiar with the intersection and he tried to retrace the trooper's movements that night northward along Stagecoach to be certain of his conclusions. He made careful on-the-scene diagrams, *(see pages 132-136)* and in his final report noted: *"There is a very wide paved shoulder on the east side of Stagecoach Road south of the intersection. Because of the width of this shoulder the STOP sign is further east than normal. When approaching the intersection from the south at night, the STOP sign at the intersection of Roosevelt Boulevard and Stagecoach Road is more visible than the STOP sign at the intersection of Tuckahoe Road and Stagecoach until a driver is 350 feet from the intersection."* That observation was to be of critical importance.

* * *

As the accident scene was being processed, other investigators were trying to get eyewitness statements. Other than those persons located immediately, it seemed no one else in the neighborhood actually saw the accident, although others heard sounds.

Lt. Eugene Taylor of the prosecutor's office joined Det. Christopher Scott of the NJSP to interview the occupants of the Mazda—Michael and his father Robert—who had been sent to Shore Memorial Hospital to be treated for any injuries. It was about 1:00 a.m. on September 28, 2006 when they interviewed Michael in the waiting room, with permission of his mother, since he was a juvenile. Michael told them he observed the "police car" approaching the intersection while they were stopped in the southbound lane. He stated the police car accelerated into the intersection and collided with the other vehicle. He stated he didn't see which direction the other vehicle was traveling prior to the collision. One of those vehicles struck the Mazda but he was not sure which. The police car struck a tree off of the roadway. He could not say why he thought it was a police car, just the style. When Det. Scott asked him how he knew the police car was accelerating, he was unable to provide any details, except to comment that it looked like he was going to stop someone.

Before leaving the hospital they also tried to interview Mr. Robert Taylor, the boy's father. Taylor said he was looking to his right, which is west, just before the collision and did not actually see the vehicles beforehand. He described one as a white vehicle and the other as "a large white object." One of the vehicles struck his car, causing the driver's side front window to shatter glass on him. Both agreed to provide more complete statements later in the day at the state police barracks.

* * *

Later the same day, before many of the witnesses could be interviewed by the police, Cape May County Prosecutor Robert Taylor received a letter from a prominent Atlantic City law firm stating that the firm was representing "the estates of Jacqueline Becker and Christina Caiafa" who were killed in a motor vehicle accident the day before," and naming the location and the state trooper involved.

The letter continued: "While the family is dealing with this horrendous tragedy, the purpose of this letter is to make sure that all physical evidence secured by the Cape May County Prosecutor's Office, including, but not limited to, all three motor vehicles are preserved for inspection at the appropriate time. I would also ask if the vehicle contained a black box that it be preserved, with its contents, and if the vehicle was video-equipped, that the tape be preserved." The law firm also promptly sent their own investigator to take statements from witnesses.

Chapter 3

Trooper Robert Higbee's huge frame hardly fit the bed as he lay on his back in an Atlantic City hospital room with his wife Beth by his side. He still seemed slightly dazed from the concussion and the pain medication for his hip, leg and back injuries. He had been in a terrible accident the night before. I had been called by the New Jersey State Troopers Fraternal Association (STFA) to represent Robert and render him legal advice. The president of the trooper's union, David Jones, had reached out for me on the morning of Thursday September 28, 2006.

Hours earlier, I had been vaguely aware from the media that there had been a fatal auto accident down in Cape May County the night before. It involved a trooper, but I knew little more from the brief news accounts. My job as an attorney was to gather the facts as best I could. I had to advise the trooper based upon anticipating possible repercussions from the incident. I had spent about thirty years in private practice and had defended many law enforcement officers in civil, criminal and administrative matters. Before my time in private practice, I had spent ten years on the prosecution side with the United States Attorney's Office in Washington, D.C. and Camden, New Jersey. I also served as an assistant prosecutor in both Camden and Atlantic County, New Jersey.

Before I had gone into private law practice, my last stint in public office included the role of police legal advisor to all police entities operating in Atlantic County. Based upon my previous experience, I believed there could certainly be serious consequences from a fatal accident while on duty. I needed to find out as quickly as possible if Higbee had done anything to impair his ability to properly perform his duty on the night of the accident.

Even though I'd just met Robert Higbee, I realized immediately that his manner and demeanor were hardly commensurate with his huge size. I could not be sure if that was simply the medication or how he normally projected himself. I could not really interview him properly in his condition. I could not get many details from him about the incident.

I was only able to get bits and pieces of the tragedy from him and more from his wife Beth. She apparently stayed by his side during the night, after she was notified by the state police to come to the hospital. When I talked with them I saw there was a uniformed trooper posted outside, perhaps sent at the request of the STFA. I believed it was for support and protection of their privacy, as there was no reason to suspect that Higbee had been placed into custody by the authorities. Beth introduced herself immediately and let me know she had gone to Holy Spirit High School in nearby Absecon with my son Daniel years before. I guessed she must be about thirty-six years old. An attractive blond haired woman, Beth was obviously distraught, but appreciated my being there for her husband. From what I learned from them, I quickly eliminated the most serious concerns I had.

Trooper Higbee had not been under the influence of alcohol, illegal drugs or medication, nor had he been sleep-deprived or otherwise impaired or distracted before the accident the night before. He had been told that two teen-aged girls had died in the accident, but he had not known them. Like me, he had grown up here in Atlantic County and was only semi-familiar with the intersection in Upper Township where the collision occurred. I could only gather that he had been trying to catch a speeder when the accident happened. I told him he needed to follow the doctor's orders, rest up and I would talk with him in more detail as he recovered. I left my card with Beth and gave the usual attorney-client warning for Robert not to talk with anyone except my investigator or me.

When I left the hospital I got approval from the STFA, to hire an investigator and had them put me in touch with the persons designated by the state police and Cape May County Prosecutor's Office to look into the matter. My immediate reaction was that this was a terrible tragedy, but no deliberate intent to cause a fatality, and no immediate information that would suggest any irresponsible or reckless conduct on the part of the trooper before the accident. Undoubtedly, there would be a civil lawsuit against the state, and possible other consequences such as motor vehicle tickets and internal discipline. But in my experience, there had been no criminal wrongdoing.

In the days following the accident the media began an incessant barrage of comments critical of Trooper Higbee, the state police, and even the prosecutor's office for not taking immediate action against the trooper. A statewide radio talk show host continuously misled his audience by claiming that the average citizen would have been arrested and thrown in jail after this incident. He called Trooper Higbee a murderer of the two girls. Picking up on the clamor, relatives and friends of the victims asked why the trooper was allowed to speed without an emergency. They wanted to know why weren't his red lights and sirens on.

I was trying to learn what really happened myself. Until Trooper Higbee recovered, I could not obtain complete details from him. I immediately notified the state police investigators and the Cape May County Prosecutor's Office of my representation of the trooper, should they wish to question him. I phoned David Meyer, the First Assistant Prosecutor in Cape May County, with whom I had dealt many times before. I also called Sgt. Karl Ulbrich of the state police whom I was told was involved taking witness statements. Neither could share what they knew so far, except to confirm the details that had been released to the media—that Higbee apparently went through the stop sign and that the girls had the right of way on Tuckahoe Road.

I had no idea what Sgt. McMahon had found, and we were not allowed to see any reports. I needed to see for myself what the intersection looked like, as we began to learn in the news accounts that there had been problems there and a number of accidents previously. An off-duty state trooper from out of the area was asked by the STFA to accompany me on a dark night similar to the conditions that prevailed on September 27. It had been less than two weeks since the accident and I wanted to know what Trooper Higbee had seen as he approached the intersection.

It was dark, and as we approached the intersection I still could not locate the stop sign because utility poles blocked the view. We had to slow down to a crawl. I was in the passenger's seat and I asked the driver to inch out into the road. We had to go past the stop line almost ten feet into the roadway before I could finally see to our right the lights of a car coming west on Tuckahoe Road. The stop sign itself was well to the right of where you would expect it, because the road was very wide at that point to allow cars to turn into the Wayside Village Shops. No wonder Robert Higbee may have had a hard time seeing the stop sign.

I got out of the car and noticed that the sign itself was not straight. Instead, it was somewhat bent, facing away from an approaching driver, and maybe that is why our lights did not illuminate it fully by reflection when we first drove up. We did not have all of the answers yet, but we knew Robert was supposed to be chasing a speeder, and maybe in driving faster than usual he made a mistake in not locating the stop sign. We finally knew we were in the right place when we looked across the road to the northwest corner and saw bunches of flowers that had been laid on the ground in memory of the two sisters..

* * *

The flowers continued to accumulate at the makeshift memorial to the girls at the intersection. Meanwhile, the family gathered together with their attorney less than two weeks after the accident to voice their concern over the length of time the investigation had taken. They also criticized the state police and Trooper Higbee for not expressing condolences and apologizing for the accident. The Cape May County prosecutor was also criticized for not taking immediate action to prosecute Trooper Higbee.

It was learned by the media that the superintendent of the state police, Col. Joseph R. Fuentes, had tried personally to express his condolences, but was advised by a family representative that the time was not appropriate. The victims' mother Maria told the press that she could not even return home because of her grief and called for answers about the cause of the accident. At the same time, two local legislators, N.J. Assemblymen Jeff Van Drew and Nelson Albano, called upon the N.J. State Department of Transportation to consider installing a traffic light at the fateful intersection.

Chief Jay Newman made the point to the media that the Chiefs' Association and the Upper Township Committee had been trying for a year to have the county do something about the "hazardous intersection," but to no avail. "I'm not a traffic safety expert," he declared. "But we responded to multiple accidents there."

It was finally revealed that the county had been waiting for the developer of a proposed new shopping center near the location, to bear the cost of installing the safety signals, but the local planning board had not required that improvement, and that nothing had been done.

While this discussion of improvements was going on, County Engineer Dale Foster was trying to make some stop-gap improvements to the intersection. He sent his road supervisor out the next day to add reflective tape on the supporting pole of the stop sign at Stagecoach and Tuckahoe Roads, but quickly decided that was not enough. He then sent out Ron Hearon, his supervisor of county traffic maintenance, to replace the existing 30-inch diameter stop sign with a larger 36-inch face, along with new red reflector poles and add yellow reflectors to the "Stop Ahead" signs.

Within about five weeks, County Engineer Foster had decided those signs were still not visible enough, so he replaced the 36-inch stop sign with a 48-inch stop sign usually used at the ends of highway exit ramps in the state. He also had the county contact the state to get an expedited traffic study. Subsequently, the county requested and obtained permission to install overhead yellow and red flashing lights over the center of the intersection. The New Jersey Department of Transportation granted permission in the fastest time that a ranking official in that department said he had ever seen. Now there were not only blinking lights and a huge stop sign, but the county additionally moved the existing street light so it would shine directly over the new stop sign.

The general public was not aware of these activities, and we mistakenly assumed that the investigators had properly photographed and documented the intersection as it had existed before all of the safety improvements were made.

In the midst of the public attention to the tragedy, I expressed our sympathies on behalf of my client and me to the family publicly. I also tried to explain that the restrictions on the trooper because of his job, and the potential liability of his employer, the state, I could not allow him to speak to anyone at this time. As soon as he was well, I expected him to give a complete statement to investigators, which he did on October 17, 2006.

Detective Sergeant Karl Ulbrich, New Jersey State Police Criminal Investigations Section (CIS), had been assigned to coordinate the witness statements for the fatal accident. He worked closely with Lt. Eugene Taylor, of the Cape May County Prosecutor's Office, who participated in all of the joint investigation interviews. Sgt. Ulbrich persistently called me to see how soon Robert Higbee would be well enough to give them his version of the incident. I talked with Ulbrich about what information he had, but all he could reveal was that there were some witnesses and preliminary analysis to suggest that Trooper Higbee could not have stopped at the stop sign before the impact. I'd surmised that much from the media accounts.

Sgt. Karl Ulbrich's job was to interview people while Sgt. McMahon was reconstructing the dynamics of the crash from the physical evidence. Ulbrich had risen through the ranks, and was known as a no-nonsense guy who knew how to extract every essential detail. He was clearly in charge when he appeared in my conference room. His closely cropped military crew cut of reddish brown hair, square jaw and monotone voice struck me as a modern-day Jack Webb who played Sgt. Friday in the old *Dragnet* television series. I imagined him to be asking for "just the facts."

Our problem was that we could not really reconstruct the moments before impact from Higbee's memory, because Higbee had no clear recollection of what took place just before and during the impact. He could not recall with any specifics how or why the crash happened. Yet his trooper's training, instincts, and sense of duty left no question in his mind that he needed to help the investigators to learn everything he could remember.

As early as October 3, Sgt. Ulbrich had heard rumors from troopers at Woodbine that a young high school student told a friend that he had been the speeder who eluded the trooper. They had not yet checked out that story. Ulbrich wanted to see what Higbee would say first. Speed estimates and interviews with the witnesses at the scene were not shared with us before the interview took place.

Before the meeting with Ulbrich and Taylor, I had spoken to Robert Higbee at length, along with his STFA union representatives, Troopers Chris Burgos and Mike Colaner. Burgos was then the vice-president of the STFA. There was nothing that we could see that suggested any criminal wrongdoing on Higbee's part, although we could not explain exactly why or how the accident happened. Colaner's experience with accident scenes made it clear that Higbee could not have come to a complete stop based upon what we knew of the crash dynamics publicly reported so far.

Yet, Robert Higbee wanted to make it clear that he was looking for a stop sign up ahead and intended to stop and look both ways before proceeding through the intersection. That is what he said he *thought* he did. He knew the protocol. If he was closing the gap on a speeder, he needed at least to slow down, and put on the overhead red lights and warning siren before going through the intersection. Sgt. Ulbrich provided Trooper Higbee with his patrol log that night to be sure he had covered every detail of his shift before the accident and he confirmed before the formal interview started, that Robert had no "personal or work related stressors" that would interfere with his concentration that night. He explored in excruciating detail everything Robert did in the twenty-four hours before the incident to be sure there was no misconduct on the trooper's part. So far, none of us believed this had been anything but a tragic motor vehicle accident, undesigned and unexpected. Robert Higbee was determined to help the investigators figure out what happened. Before recording the interview, Ulbrich and Taylor read Higbee the required Miranda Rights. We then waived his rights to refuse to incriminate himself. After all, Higbee needed to cooperate with the authorities, and we believed he did not commit any criminal wrongdoing.

Robert Higbee related everything he could remember, but moments before the crash he was unable to recollect seeing either the Beckers' van, or any other vehicle at the intersection. Although he thought he had stopped and looked both ways, he conceded he might have mistaken the driveway to the Frito Lay warehouse for Tuckahoe Road. He never saw anything in his way before the crash. He was focused on the taillights of the speeder up ahead. Then there was "darkness" and he woke up realizing he had been in an accident. His entire testimony under oath on October 17, 2006 was filled with phrases like: "as best I can remember" and "to the best I can recall." To an experienced investigator, these are tip-offs that the subject does not have clear recall of what happened.

Sgt. Ulbrich did not believe Higbee was concealing anything or attempting to deceive him. Higbee told Taylor and Ulbrich in the pre-interview that he was not "hell-bent" on catching the speeder, so there would be no reason for him not to have stopped or at least slowed down considerably before passing the stop sign. After all, troopers don't get promotions based upon speeding tickets. In fact, warnings are encouraged when possible. But Ulbrich knew what witness statements he had, and the Fatal Accident Unit's measurements suggested that the minimum speed of the patrol car was such that Higbee could not have come to a complete stop and create the energy necessary for the resulting crash dynamics. More work needed to be done to find out what had caused this tragedy, even if Higbee did not know all of the answers.

When Trooper Higbee recovered sufficiently, his boss, Col. J.R. "Rick" Fuentes, superintendent of the state police, permitted him to return to the state police on light duty, which is administrative desk duty, until the accident investigation could be completed. He could have suspended Higbee without pay, but there was no reason to do that because there appeared to be no deliberate misconduct on the part of the trooper, and Higbee would not be required to go back on road patrol at this time.

On October 23, 2006, Cape May County Prosecutor Robert Taylor, an appointee of the former Democratic governor, called a meeting. Taylor had held his office for a five-year term until reappointed and confirmed by the New Jersey Senate. To avoid missing the thirty-day statute of limitations for motor vehicle offenses, Taylor and First Assistant Prosecutor J. David Meyer, ordered the state police commanders at the meeting to issue summonses to Trooper Higbee, citing him for failure to yield at the stop sign, and for careless driving—two traffic offenses commonly punished by fines and possibly suspension of driving privileges. These would be handled at the lowest municipal court level since they were traffic tickets and not considered criminal offenses. Not even the more serious traffic offense of reckless driving was merited according to the prosecutor.

Sgt. Ulbrich promptly arranged for me to accept service of the traffic tickets for Trooper Higbee the next day. I informed the court and prosecutor that I would represent Higbee when the matter could be heard. I knew that the prosecutor, because of the fatalities, would hold the case open until the conclusion of the investigation. That same day, Sgt. Ulbrich and Lt. Eugene Taylor were able to track down and talk with Josh Wigglesworth at Ocean City High School.

The next day, with his mother's permission Josh gave them a formal statement confirming his involvement as the speeder. Prosecutor Taylor never admitted to the media that he had a sworn statement from Josh, so many reporters continued to speculate that the speeder was a "phantom," suggesting that Higbee had no reason to be exceeding the limit that night. But both Sergeants Ulbrich and McMahon were able to corroborate the accounts of Higbee and Wigglesworth by returning to the scene and recreating the descriptions. They concluded that Wigglesworth would have been able to see the accident in his rear view mirror as he approached the stop sign at Roosevelt, and Higbee could have seen Wigglesworth's lights illuminating the stop sign at the intersection beyond him.

We did not know what the investigators knew at that time. But we soon learned of the intervention of the law firm representing the girls' family. The firm hired a private investigator who filed a citizen's complaint against Higbee in the Upper Township Municipal Court, for reckless driving, as we later learned. Also unknown to us at the time, the law firm had continued to press the prosecutor's office to obtain downloaded data from the patrol car's electronic data recorder, known as an event data recorder (EDR). All I found out in the next few months was that the prosecutor was dealing with Ford Motor Company to obtain downloaded information about pre-crash speed, acceleration and braking of the police vehicle. Even so, I saw no deliberate misconduct on the part of the trooper.

Both McMahon and Ulbrich concluded that the trooper was justified in exceeding the speed limit without lights and sirens to attempt to catch Wigglesworth, even though he may have committed motor vehicle violations in failing to yield or put on emergency lights at the stop sign. I did not know it, but reports by Ulbrich and McMahon were practically complete by the end of December 2006. They never suggested any misconduct by Higbee beyond the traffic violations. But any final conclusions had to come from the Cape May County prosecutor.

I kept checking with First Assistant Prosecutor David Meyer into January of 2007 to see when the matter could be concluded. I fully expected that there might be some civil ramifications, an appearance in municipal court and perhaps even an imposed brief suspension by the state police, if Robert lost his driving privileges. I wanted to resolve everything as quickly as possible so that Robert could return to full duties after any administrative disposition. I anticipated that the family would recover financial damages from the State of New Jersey in a civil court, for any fault by the trooper, because he was on duty at the time of the accident.

The family and their lawyers held a press conference, causing some members of the media to accuse the authorities of a cover-up and demanding justice. I understood the emotional outpouring of the family, but I felt the criticism of the delay was unwarranted because the prosecutor was seeking material they had demanded from Ford to complete the accident reconstruction. In any case, I did not see that any further charges against Higbee were justified. No matter what penalties were imposed upon Higbee, New Jersey would inevitably pay damages to the family for the accident.

As a lawyer I was perplexed. What possible motivation could there be to see Robert Higbee prosecuted for a criminal offense? If he had deliberately caused an accident, the state would disclaim liability and would refuse to pay damages for the wrongdoing. If Robert went to jail, the girls' family could not collect any financial damages from him. To me, it seemed obvious that Higbee was doing his duty and that this had been a tragic accident.

That is, so I thought, until February 2007, when Cape May County Prosecutor Robert Taylor converted the case from an accident to a crime. And he did so without even informing the state police's lead investigators that he intended to take the case to a Grand Jury to seek an Indictment.

Chapter 4

By early 2007, we were satisfied that Trooper Robert Higbee was not an irresponsible individual who would deliberately risk lives and did not consciously make a decision to ignore the stop sign on September 27, 2006. However, despite the continued pressure from the media, Prosecutor Taylor would only confirm that his criminal investigation had not concluded. In a press release in early January, he referred to witnesses' statements, in which they denied ever seeing a speeder ahead of the trooper.

Taylor never told the media about Josh Wigglesworth's sworn statement. He never stated publicly that investigators physically corroborated accounts of the speeder and Higbee by retracing the scene, proving Higbee's reasonable on-duty conduct attempting to catch Wigglesworth.

Was there behind the scenes pressure to prosecute Higbee by the highly connected civil law firm hired by the victims' family? Was Prosecutor Taylor concerned about his reappointment when his term of office expired? We may never know what motivated the Cape May Prosecutor.

What we did know is the prosecutor seemed to be relying upon the EDR data from the trooper's 2005 Ford Crown Victoria, which he apparently had received in January 2007. The STFA had allowed me to retain my longtime Investigator Manny Ridgeway, a lanky retired state police detective, who lived in the Cape May area. We had found out as much as we could of the incident. However, we now needed to learn everything about the device inside the Ford that might provide detailed measurements of pre-impact speed and braking. In November 2006, we hired Lt. Barry Wythe, a consultant who was an accident reconstructionist. He had recently retired after more than twenty years of law enforcement. He had investigated hundreds of fatal accidents for the Atlantic County Prosecutor, and before that, as a sergeant in the Egg Harbor Township Police. He told us the Ford device would simply corroborate more precisely the findings of the State Police Fatal Accident Unit.

There was still no reason to think Robert Higbee was reckless because there was nothing in the pre-impact history to suggest impairment. All of Wythe's previous cases involved some deliberate unjustified action of a driver before the impact, such as consumption of alcohol or drugs, sleep deprivation, cell phone distraction, or drag racing for example. No police officer had ever been indicted criminally for this situation. Nonetheless we now needed to be prepared for whatever this prosecutor might do. The media involvement suddenly escalated about the time we worried that the Prosecutor was really thinking of taking this case to a Grand Jury. Not only were the local press, TV and radio hammering Higbee, but we also heard of possible national interest in the case.

I kept getting calls from an assistant producer from the ABC network show *20/20*. She wanted to interview Trooper Higbee for an upcoming segment they intended to air about the accident. I declined on behalf of my client, since we had conferred and agreed it was inappropriate in view of pending motor vehicle charges and the ongoing investigation. But I finally agreed to provide information myself. With the help of the Trooper's Union, we would explain the procedures that justified the trooper's conduct in not using red lights and sirens prior to the stop. ABC's focus was ostensibly questioning the protocols. The staff of *20/20* insisted they wanted to be objective, since the victims' family, some witnesses, and even the Cape May Prosecutor's Office had already agreed to be interviewed. I reluctantly agreed to go to New York City along with several STFA representatives, to protect the trooper's interest. Only in hindsight, after the taped segment aired, would we really be able to speculate on *20/20*'s motivation for this broadcast.

The STFA President David Jones and Vice-president Chris Burgos had extensive experience with the media on behalf of troopers.

Jones, with a forceful New York accent and outgoing personality, can best be described as feisty. Chris is a bit more reserved, but an imposing figure, tireless in his protection of the membership. Both warned me that the TV show probably had an agenda, which might well be to portray law enforcement as being uncaring and reckless in the performance of duties. Why else would this case be of any national interest?

We drove together into New York City to ABC, located beyond Columbus Circle between Broadway and Central Park West. The building was a maze of interconnected hallways with various studios. The producers quickly made it clear they did not want to discuss anything or rehearse, but rather needed to interview Jones and me "cold" so there could be no opportunity to confer or prepare for their questions. That really did not matter to us. We had all done our research on the law and the state police protocols long beforehand, and did not need to hear what each other said. Jones would be interviewed first, and I went over to the news side to visit with ABC News Anchor Charles Gibson, who had gone to Sidwell Friends School with my wife in Washington, D.C.

Gibson was not at all involved with 20/20. He graciously showed me around his offices and we talked while I was waiting. The substance of our conversation was not about this case.

About an hour or so later I was called back by 20/20 for the interview. I was ushered right into a brightly-lit set where the staff was putting more makeup on the 20/20 interviewer Bill Ritter. The producer wanted to be sure I had not spoken with Jones, so they immediately started taping.

I answered every question Ritter posed. I tried valiantly to explain why the fatal accident was not a criminal matter. I said the key element in a vehicular homicide case would have to be proof beyond a reasonable doubt of reckless conduct on the part of the trooper. There had been no conscious disregard of human life, or gross deviation from what a reasonable person would have done under all of the circumstances. Higbee was a trooper obliged to do his duty and there was an accident. It could have happened to anybody.

Ritter wanted to debate the state police procedure as to why Higbee's red lights and sirens were not on. He kept calling the action a "pursuit" which was incorrect. Higbee was actually "closing the gap" on the speeder, whom he had not yet been able to identify. He could not even make out the license plate. A pursuit would be if the trooper had signaled the driver to stop, and then he tried to elude the officer. Entirely different police procedures apply. Ritter did not seem terribly interested in my answers or in any explanations. Soon the hour was up and we were heading back to South Jersey. We had little hope that we would receive fair treatment by the show, but we had tried.

The next morning, February 22, 2007, I was informed that Assistant Prosecutor David Meyer was intending to present the Higbee case to a Cape May County grand jury. I immediately went to Cape May Court House with Barry Wythe to discuss the matter in person with Meyer. On the phone, Meyer made it clear he was not attempting to get the grand jury to return a "No Bill," that is, rule that no criminal prosecution was warranted. To the contrary, Meyer suggested the EDR data, which I had not seen, might provide evidence of criminal conduct, which could produce a "True Bill," that is an indictment against Trooper Higbee. Wythe and I arrived at the prosecutor's office in Cape May Court House (the actual name of the town). The main prosecutor's office consists of a group of metal buildings connected together, but looking like they were temporarily put up years before, and never replaced by permanent structures. They are actually in Middle Township, about a mile or so from the actual court house. Meyer took us right into his private office.

Without revealing any details of the EDR data, Meyer strongly suggested that Robert Higbee knew or should have known the exact location of the stop sign. Meyer claimed Higbee consciously disregarded it, and was traveling too fast into the intersection to avoid the impact. He implied that when Higbee turned right on to Stagecoach Road he should have remembered seeing the dull gray tin reverse side of the stop sign. He said Higbee should have noted its location in his mind before he turned around to go back north. We protested that was an absurd conclusion. No normal driver, even a policeman takes particular note of the backside of a sign as he turns onto a street. We could not conceive of any reason why the trooper would consciously decide to ignore the stop sign.

We told Meyer neither Wythe nor I knew of any case in New Jersey where a police officer had ever been charged criminally under these circumstances. We were extremely concerned about the prosecutor's intentions, but we seemed unable to persuade Meyer there was absolutely no basis for a criminal indictment of Higbee. Less than a week later, our worst fears were realized. The long nightmare for Robert Higbee and all of us began on February 27, 2007. We learned five months to the day after the accident that Trooper Robert Higbee had been indicted by a grand jury on two counts of vehicular homicide, punishable by a combined total exposure of 20 years in prison if convicted.

Cape May County Prosecutor Robert Taylor had his day with the media on February 27, 2007. He held a press conference to announce Trooper Higbee's indictment on two counts of vehicular homicide, serious second-degree crimes. The rotund, red-faced prosecutor with a bushy gray mustache and wire rimmed glasses stood before the cameras and microphones to make his announcement. To my knowledge that was the last time he showed his face in public to talk about this case. He left the details of the prosecution after that to First Assistant Prosecutor J. David Meyer.

The Trooper's Union President David Jones wasted no time in responding. His press release expressed profound sorrow for the loss of the two girls, and repeated all of our sympathies for the family for their loss. But Jones pointed out that Higbee was fully in compliance with all police requirements and was performing his duties. The accident was woefully devastating, but not a crime. The decision of the Cape May prosecutor to indict, "flies in the face" of all of the known statutes, precedents and case law in New Jersey, exclaimed Jones.

"It sends a message to everyone in law enforcement, that despite the rules that are in place, if you make an honest but tragic mistake, you will be fighting for your freedom for trying to do your job." He promised publicly and privately the full resources of the STFA to defend Trooper Higbee's innocence. The outspoken leader of the troopers said what I was thinking, but I could not say, because of the restrictions of the Attorneys' Rules of Professional Conduct.

Rob Higbee and I tried to absorb what we faced in order to defend him. I had to be more reserved in my public remarks, and focused on the law, to try to explain why his conduct was not "reck-less" and he should not be facing criminal charges. This was a tragic and unfortunate accident, but I said the matter does not belong in criminal court. Higbee was doing his sworn duty and never deliberately disregarded or endangered a human life. We extended our sympathy to the family but maintained that, "Trooper Higbee is innocent of any criminal act." Predictably the media from New York through South Jersey to Philadelphia blasted the trooper and showed gruesome depictions of the fatal accident. The victims' family held a news conference at their lawyer's offices in Atlantic City. Their lawyer said the trooper's actions had nothing to do with chasing a speeder, calling that "totally irrelevant."

Davy Jones correctly predicted the reaction of the law enforcement community nationwide: "No trooper, no police officer should be offered up for political expediency because of a horrible, but very human mistake. The convoluted message this is sending to honest, hardworking cops who are just trying their best to do their job with the plethora of problems and obstacles that it already comes with it, cannot be understated. The chilling effect on law enforcement and the public we serve will be monumental."

Chapter 5

*R*emorse is a term often considered by a judge when sentencing a criminal defendant to determine if he has appreciated the wrongful conduct that led to the tragic consequences of his act. I maintain that term is inappropriate in this context. Trooper Robert Higbee expressed deep regret that his actions set in motion the circumstances, which contributed to the deaths of two young girls. He felt the sorrow, the compassion, and understood the awful void left in the lives of the parents and grandparents of Jacqueline and Christina. But he knew in his heart that he never had any intention for them to die. He was simply doing his duty. He never wanted to see any innocent person hurt. He wanted to come home to his wife uninjured that night. He would not have risked his own life to catch a speeder.

Why did the prosecutor think he should go to prison for trying to do his duty that night? First Assistant Prosecutor David Meyer had been on the job for many years. He was middle aged, somewhat balding, relatively short in stature, but taller than I am. He appears to be carefully groomed, polished and meticulous, commensurate with his trial preparation. He is a very formidable adversary because of his careful attention to detail in his preparation. Yet, I still could not figure out what he might have in his undisclosed evidence to convince a jury that Robert Higbee was a criminal in this case.

I immediately started the process to question why the indictment was returned. On March 15, 2007 the formal process began. Fortunately, Meyer understood Higbee would show up for his trial, and did not require him to be arrested and handcuffed. Instead we arranged for Higbee to surrender his badge and gun, be fingerprinted and photographed at the Woodbine state police barracks. He would then appear when notified to come to court. We came with Rob's family members and his supporters from all of the law enforcement community that day to enter his not guilty plea before the court. When the indictment was announced Higbee was immediately suspended without pay and benefits by the Superintendent of the state police. Chris Burgos, the vice president of the STFA, drove us all to the court in his own private SUV.

We came in the back door to the courthouse to try to minimize the crush of media. The Cape May courthouse is a brick structure with four ionic columns in the front, standing in contrast to the old courthouse next door, which looked like a little white church and was just used for ceremonial events. The current courtrooms are somewhat modern and sterile. Superior Court Judge Carmen Alvarez presided over the arraignment proceedings. She appeared satisfied with the prosecutor's recommendation that bail would not be necessary to assure Higbee's appearance in court again. The judge, gray-haired and with glasses, was a somewhat soft-spoken, but generally stern and matter-of-fact judge, long serving on the criminal bench in Cape May County.

We entered the perfunctory not guilty plea, and requested discovery of all relevant evidence from the prosecutor. We particularly asked for the so-called "black box" data from the Ford Crown Victoria and the recorded proceedings of Meyer's presentation to the Cape May grand jury that resulted in the indictment. After the judge left the bench, I approached the family's lawyer as requested by my client. Rob wanted to meet the victims' mother to express his sympathies and concern. Up to now he had not been permitted to have any contact with Maria Caiafa. As agreed, the tall trooper, dressed in a gray suit, blue shirt, and yellow tie, approached the grieving mother. She was somber and looked haggard with deep rings under her eyes. Her dark hair hung limply over her dark clothing as she looked up to Higbee.

As they engaged in a brief and quiet conversation, Maria Caiafa then reached up and hugged Rob in an emotional and tearful embrace *(see page 146)*. It was a brief moment in time, but for those of us who were nearby, including her father Caesar Caiafa, there were genuine tears. Rob had expressed regret and sorrow for her loss and the hug was an indication that she accepted his sincere concern. I never remember a similar event in a criminal case, where the victim's loved one could express that feeling openly. She hugged the man she held responsible for the death of her daughters. It was not forgiveness, but it was her acceptance that he really felt sorry for her loss.

Her attorney was later to praise the effort, hoping it would aid in the grieving and healing process for Maria. In the months that followed, I was to learn even more about the strong, but compassionate character and temperament of Rob Higbee. I found out about him from friends, family, and other public servants. Since I had only known Rob since our first meeting in the hospital, I discretely asked others to tell me about him. I knew that if we ever had to go to trial he probably would have to testify in his own behalf. His willingness to reach out to Maria Caiafa despite her condemnation of him and the state police in the media said a lot about him.

I spoke to Bill Advena, a longtime friend of mine, who had been a classmate in Atlantic City High School many years ago. Bill is a retired Mainland High School science teacher. He had Rob Higbee as a student and also watched him in sports at Mainland. Bill speaks his mind without hesitation or sugarcoating his remarks. He is not given to superlatives and is sometimes brutally honest to the point of insult. Yet he said to me: "If you could choose a son you would want to choose Rob Higbee."

Others later echoed that description. None of his supervisors, past employers, co-workers, or even athletes who played against him had anything negative to say about him. Because of the extreme publicity generated about his case, I tried to avoid putting Rob in public scrutiny. I even avoided bringing him in to our Atlantic City law offices, because the firm representing the Caiafa/Becker family had their offices in the same building. Many times I had Rob come to my house to review documents and to meet with Investigator Ridgeway and me.

Soon after he began to meet with me at my home, my wife, Petie, pulled me aside after he left and pointedly told me: "You'd better do your best to represent him." She clearly believed in him very strongly as well. It was obvious Higbee was not an individual with any criminal intent. He would never decide to engage in reckless conduct. He agonized over the deaths. He was innocent of Vehicular Homicide. But now it was up to me to see that he was found not guilty.

The pressing legal issues quickly put the emotional embrace between the bereaved mother and the accused defendant aside. We needed to find out what had been presented to the grand jury and what information was relevant from the numbers stored in the so-called black box in the trooper's car.

As attorneys for Rob Higbee we were on our own except for any support we could get from the STFA. Rob no longer had any income from the state police. We immediately asked the state attorney general to provide for his legal defense according to the discretion permitted under State law, since Higbee was in the performance of his duties at the time of the accident.

The attorney general declined, stating in effect if Higbee were ultimately acquitted of all criminal charges we could then apply for reimbursement of legal fees and costs. In other words, the State cut off all pay, benefits and support for the trooper. That approach sounded to me like presumed guilty instead of presumed innocent. Fortunately, the troopers' union stepped up and advanced costs so we could quickly order the transcripts of the grand jury proceeding. As soon as we got some preliminary data from the EDR, investigator Barry Wythe and I went up to consult with a nationally recognized accident reconstruction and EDR expert, W.R. "Rusty" Haight, of the Collision Safety Institute of San Diego, California. Fortunately, we were able to meet him at a break from a seminar he was teaching in North Jersey.

I learned that the State had originally sought Ford Motor Company's help in getting data from the patrol car and a formal request for Ford to download the data had been made in December of 2006, as a result of a deal with Ford's General Counsel in Michigan. Apparently the information was contained in two separate mechanisms in the Ford police cruiser: a restraint control module (RCM) to measure when safety bags deployed, and a power control module (PCM), to measure systems such as acceleration and braking prior to impact. While General Motors vehicles had similar devices producing that information, those were contained in a single unit. GM information had been used, but there had been no case utilizing the Ford data in our courts. Ford had not released the software to allow anyone outside of its company to read the data. The original purpose was to monitor safety and systems for Ford's use and was not designed to provide information to be used in cases like this one.

In addition we learned the data still had to be used in conjunction with an opinion of an expert who was qualified in accident reconstruction, like Sgt. McMahon, Wythe, and Haight himself. There were problems with what the prosecutor provided to us. We knew from on scene investigation that Higbee's air bag had deployed, but the RCM in his car did not show that, probably because the power to the device was cut off the moment the battery and electrical system failed with the collision. Also, there were multiple impacts, and it was not clear at which point the device stopped recording. The prosecutor alleged that the PCM accurately showed 25 seconds of pre-impact information.

We really did not know how reliable the Ford data was, or even if it was admissible in a New Jersey court. From the grand jury transcript we learned the only witness produced by the Cape May prosecutor's office was its own Lieutenant of Detectives, Eugene Taylor. He simply paraphrased and summarized all of the reports and documents he read for his testimony. Not a single report, photograph or document was ever shown to the grand jury. Moreover, Taylor had testified Trooper Higbee never went below 70 miles per hour before the final 1.2 seconds before the impact when he hit the brakes.

That was contradicted by the actual EDR data and Sgt. McMahon's analysis. Even more disturbing to us, not one word of the terrible configuration of the intersection was told to the grand jurors. They never learned of the twenty-six prior accidents there, nor were they told of all of the upgraded safety changes added after the fatalities. Worse yet, we read in the transcript that a grand juror asked the prosecutor why Higbee was speeding if he was not "hell-bent" on catching the speeder. The prosecutor answered: "That he knows...he alone knows that..." The prosecutor never explained why the trooper had to accelerate faster than the speeder to try to apprehend him after turning around and beginning from a complete stop after his K-turn. The prosecutor was asked to "read from the book," meaning the statutes, to explain the definition of "recklessness." Instead of reading what the case law requires, "a gross deviation from that which a reasonable person" would do under all of the circumstances, the prosecutor added his own spin; he said Higbee's conduct should be measured by the standard of a "reasonable law enforcement officer."

We thought that held the trooper to some higher standard of care. Finally, we discovered the prosecutor never explained the difference from the commonly understood "careless" standard which was not criminal, but just a traffic violation. He told the grand jurors the law imposed upon Higbee "an even greater obligation to be cautious and circumspect as he's approaching an intersection." He never told them what, if anything, Higbee should have done or could have done given the probability that he could not see the stop sign at the poorly marked intersection. Neither Sgt. McMahon nor Sgt. Ulbrich was called to testify, nor were their reports shown to the jury.

The grand jurors were left to speculate why red lights and siren were not on, and were never told the difference between a "pursuit" and "closing the gap" with a violator. When a grand juror asked the prosecutor in effect whether the injuries might not have been fatal had the passenger worn her seat belt, the prosecutor stated that was something that was "debatable." My investigator told me clearly the impact within the compartment would not have proved fatal if the passenger's seat belt was on.

I pointed out all of these discrepancies in a lengthy legal brief and argument to Judge Alvarez, but she denied the motion to dismiss the indictment in June of 2007.

* * *

The case had begun to gnaw at my insides like a creeping ulcer. What could I do to halt the process leading to the uncertainty of a jury trial? About a week or so after our first court appearance, *20/20* broadcast the TV segment about the accident on ABC's national network. The show was as one-sided as the prosecutor's presentation to the grand jury. Not one word of my interview was aired, and only a few moments of David Jones' were shown. None of our explanations of the law or state police procedures were given, even after we spent so much time with *20/20* in New York. My only two words consisted of a voice-over from court, when I entered the plea of "Not Guilty" on behalf of my client. Anyone watching the show would have seen only heart-rending interviews with the grieving family and speculation by witnesses that there was no speeder.

The lead-in to the TV show practically accused Higbee of being the murderer of the two young girls. The widespread negative publicity increased my concern about getting a fair trial by a jury that had not already been tainted. Meantime, I agonized over the legal issues involved. I filed motions to preclude evidence of the EDR data, and still could not figure out why the prosecutor thought he could prove a criminal state of mind. I began to doubt my own analysis and sought help from friends and colleagues all over the state.

One meeting brought me north to Ocean County to a secret conference where I sat with a retired superior court judge, a retired county prosecutor, and the STFA representatives in the law offices of an attorney who was himself a former trooper. All agreed I was correct in my thinking and ultimately I should prevail as a matter of law. However, the Cape May Court rulings continued to deny any relief. More motions were argued during the summertime as we began to get calls, emails, and messages from all over the country that police and emergency responders were concerned about the bad precedent if Higbee were to go to jail for an honest misperception in a fraction of a second.

I had Barry Wythe search the country for competent experts on the Ford Motor Company EDR. He had several communications and a long phone conversation with a retired Ford Engineer named Richard Ruth about the case. However, at this time we could not hire him because the prosecutor still had not supplied us with a written Opinion Report from his own EDR Expert. I also had Manny Ridgeway try to find everything he could about the credibility of the witness statements and to learn all we could about the intersection before the changes had been made.

During this same time I was battling the office of the Attorney General of New Jersey, Anne Milgram. Her office had refused to even provide a defense for Trooper Higbee to the complaint filed in civil court against him and the state police by the family seeking money damages for the car accident. The state was obligated by law to represent Higbee because his conduct was on duty. But the attorney general wanted to wait to see what would happen to him in the criminal case first. After months of paperwork, calls, and discussions with the civil courts, I was finally able to persuade the attorney general to appear for Higbee and take over the civil case. However, this was only with the understanding that if he were found guilty in criminal court the state would refuse to be responsible for anything. There could be a huge judgment for money damages against Higbee in addition to imprisonment.

Not only did Higbee have to seek outside employment on a temporary basis to feed his family, with no money for his legal defense in the criminal case, but he might also get hit with a personal judgment for damages even if he was acquitted of criminal charges. His personal car insurance would not cover the accident, because his employer, the State of New Jersey should have been responsible for him while driving a patrol car on duty. To fill the temporary gap in resources, Rob's brothers and sisters in the state police got together on their own time for fund raisers to try to help the STFA in support of Rob. I even appealed to our intermediate court, the appellate division of superior court for help, but a ruling on this issue was deemed premature. If Rob was found not guilty, I could come back for relief against the attorney general to provide him with monetary reimbursement if he could survive that long.

As to the appeal from Judge Alvarez's denial of my motion to dismiss the indictment, after submitting over 500 pages of documentation, my one word answer from the court where I sought Interlocutory relief was: "Denied." I really was not surprised. The appellate court would not throw out the charges at this stage. Very seldom does a higher court intervene for the defense in a criminal case.

The reason is the defense has "two bites at the apple." A mistake by the trial court can be corrected on appeal after a conviction, but double jeopardy precludes correction of trial error if the State's evidence is not allowed. So the only appeals, which are normally granted before a trial takes place, are in favor of the prosecution. We were forced to try the case; if we lost, we could appeal the conviction.

I had also obtained information that there had been 179 fatal accidents at New Jersey stop signs in the four years before this 2006 incident, and none had resulted in vehicular homicide charges in the state, unless the driver was impaired or deliberately reckless as in drag racing, for example. Because each county prosecutor brings criminal cases, I had to subpoena records from all twenty-one counties to show the trial judge this case was the first of its kind in the state.

The prosecutor moved to reject the subpoenaed evidence and the judge agreed, calling it a mere "fishing expedition." I lost again. By the end of the summer of 2007, Judge Alvarez had been elevated to the appellate division herself, and the case was reassigned to the Honorable Raymond Batten, judge of the superior court, for the criminal trial.

Chapter 6

Judge Raymond Batten is tall, balding, with wispy blond hair. When on the bench he sometimes peers down over half-glasses for reading. In his mid-fifties, he still maintains somewhat of an athletic appearance from his undergraduate rowing on the Princeton University Crew. He was a former Assemblyman and former municipal prosecutor for several municipalities in Cape May County before being named to the bench in 1996. He had seemed fair and objective in my past dealings with him. He had a reputation for patiently listening to the arguments from both sides.

In the fall of 2007 with Judge Alvarez on the higher court, Judge Batten was handling all of the criminal cases in the county. Recognizing the importance of this case, Judge Batten called Mr. Meyer and me together to confer on scheduling and tried to have us outline all of the issues that should be decided before the trial began. My most immediate concern was the lack of an expert report on the EDR from the prosecutor. Meyer had supplied some raw data downloaded from the device by an engineer at Ford Motor Company in Dearborn, Michigan, named Orin West, but his credentials had not been furnished to us.

We still had no written report to anticipate Mr. West's trial testimony. Judge Batten promptly ordered the prosecutor to comply with all of our discovery requests, but had to adjourn the motion we had filed almost five months ago before Judge Alvarez to decide if the state was even going to be able to introduce the Ford EDR data for the first time in New Jersey. We could not argue the same motions decided against us by Judge Alvarez, but we again brought up some of the discrepancies in the grand jury presentation, especially the misinformation given to them about the EDR. Our expert, Mr. Haight, had written the description and evaluation of the EDR given to the grand jurors by Lt. Taylor was "at best, incomplete, at worst, in places misrepresented."

We were entitled to know who was going to testify against us, and what each witness would say at trial. We also learned that the prosecutor had spent more taxpayers' money to procure two reports from a firm in Oklahoma known as Jackson Hole Scientific Investigations, Inc., in an effort to supplement or perhaps replace the accident reconstruction done by NJSP Sgt. McMahon. It turned out those experts agreed with McMahon's findings and even commended him for his work. Maybe that is why Meyer decided not to use them for trial. We saw their report mentioned articles written by both Orin West and Richard Ruth, who apparently had worked together at Ford before Ruth retired earlier that year.

In the fall of 2007 and the beginning of 2008 we were still pushing for Orin West's report so we could hire our own expert. Finally, it was revealed to the judge and me that Mr. Meyer had been unable to persuade Ford Motor Company to voluntarily produce Orin West as an expert for the criminal trial. To my astonishment, the prosecutor then requested Judge Batten to order Mr. West to provide a report and come to New Jersey from Michigan to testify. An expert is usually a person who agrees to write a report, and testify for a fee. West worked for Ford, and as its employee, could not testify regarding Ford's products without the company's permission. Ford Motor Company's General Counsel in Michigan quickly hired a New Jersey law firm to come into court and argue against the prosecutor's motion to compel Mr. West to appear. Moreover, Ford resisted production of documents we requested to test the reliability of this downloaded data from the PCM to be used against us in the case. We learned from Paul Russell, Ford's New Jersey attorney, that the company was unwilling to have its employees used in this manner to support prosecutions around the country based upon its EDR data.

We finally got some of what we wanted and were allowed to look at other documents from Ford with a Protective Order from the judge. We could not make those public because the information was proprietary and Ford did not want to reveal their secrets to competitors. Judge Batten agreed with the Ford attorneys and me that there was no legal basis for him to order Ford to produce Orin West for trial testimony. Now, more than a year after indictment, the prosecutor could not even supply an expert witness on the EDR even though that data was primarily what he relied upon to convince the grand jury to indict Higbee.

In one of the many court appearances before Judge Batten, I expressed frustration that my client was still suspended without pay awaiting the trial. Higbee's life was on hold waiting for the prosecutor. I said in open court that we had already searched the country for experts and questioned why the prosecution was unable to find one. I also mentioned that for example we had even spoken to retired Ford Engineer Richard Ruth.

Little did I know at that time, but Ruth's friends from Ford, upon learning of the judge's decision, sent Ruth the article with the court's ruling. Ruth sent an email to First Assistant Prosecutor Meyer in less than a week saying if he needed an expert to replace Orin West in the case, "I am your best choice." We found out later that Meyer hired him despite knowing Ruth had previously consulted with us on this very case. We moved to disqualify Ruth on that basis, but the judge ruled that we had not paid Ruth any money yet, so the state was free to hire him against us.

While we were delayed waiting for the EDR Report now expected from Ruth, we finally got a slight glimmer of hope that all of the public opinion had not yet been swayed in favor of the prosecution. An accident had happened in Atlantic County involving a police officer responding to an emergency who failed to immediately slow down upon notification of a downgrade in the call's priority. An intersection fatality took place but the officer was dealt with administratively and civilly and not charged criminally by the Atlantic County Prosecutor. The local newspaper, *The Press of Atlantic City*, wrote an editorial, which thought that the officer should face more severe administrative action, but agreed neither the officer nor Trooper Higbee should face criminal charges. As to Higbee, the editorial stated, "putting Higbee on trial in the criminal courts seems to us to be a perversion of justice."

In stating Higbee is "being treated too harshly," the editorial stated it would not speculate on whether the publicity compelled the Cape May prosecutor to exercise his discretion to seek an indictment against Higbee. But "sending Higbee to prison would be a miscarriage of justice."

Maybe there was hope for a fair trial after all.

* * *

Putting Rob Higbee through a criminal trial by jury seemed unjust and unfair. But now it seemed inevitable. Whatever we had to do to prepare for trial we did for the rest of 2008. Our resources were limited. I worked for a law firm that was used to getting paid every thirty days by corporate and municipal clients. I got paid only if the clients paid. Rob struggled just to take care of his family with interim jobs for friends and helping to train athletes. Because he had to commit to being in court for every motion and for the upcoming trial, no one would hire him on a regular basis. It was clear he intended to return to the state police if found not guilty. Higbee soon had to turn to unemployment benefits. I was forced to resign from the law firm and tried to make it on my own, because I was determined to defend Rob.

I fit in work for paying clients whenever I was not preparing for the Higbee trial. With help from the STFA we sought experts. For investigation and preparation we relied a lot upon volunteers. I was teaching part time as an Adjunct Professor of Criminal Justice at the Richard Stockton College of New Jersey, in addition to my law practice. A faculty colleague, who is also a lawyer, Robert Herman, supplied me with some legal research. I met a retired police officer, Lou Horvath, who was working a security position at the building where my classes were held. He went on the Internet on his own time and gave me volumes of material and contacts he found to learn more about the EDR.

As a result, I had long telephone consultations with Professor Tom Kowalick in North Carolina, who provided valuable insights into the device, again for no charge. We still needed the state's expert report almost sixteen months after the indictment. On June 4,

2008, we suddenly got the call from Prosecutor David Meyer that we could come observe a new download of the PCM data from the trooper's car if we came to his office that night. I quickly arranged for Barry Wythe and Manny Ridgeway to meet me at the Cape May prosecutor's office. It was a dark, rainy and stormy night when we arrived. The prosecutor had flown in Richard Ruth from Michigan. We saw Ruth immediately as self-centered, arrogant and smug. He was disheveled in his appearance.

Ruth perfunctorily went through the motions of retrieving the information so he could testify to an independent analysis, and the prosecutor would not need Orin West at all. We were there just to see that he followed correct procedures and that the numbers he was going to rely upon were taken from the little metal device removed from the state police 2005 Crown Victoria. It was all for show. Ruth had his report to the prosecutor within a week. He probably knew what he was going to put in the report that night. We did not learn until much later, that Ruth combined his trip to Cape May with his attendance at a seminar in Westchester, Pennsylvania, a little more than 60 miles away.

It turns out he wanted to bolster his credentials by taking a quick course on "Human Factors" in automobile accidents, since his past experience with only a B.S. in Electrical Engineering from Michigan Tech did not provide him with that expertise. He had never done an accident reconstruction on his own either. He needed to quickly bootstrap his credentials to help the prosecutor. The Ruth Report, produced a week after his visit to Cape May, also had a disclaimer attached. He warned that Ford had developed the RCM for information on restraint device, not for accident reconstruction. The time series deceleration data from the PCM may not necessarily be the speed of the vehicle pre-crash. All the data retrieved must be compared with professional accident reconstruction.

The Ruth Report, therefore, could not stand alone. The prosecutor still needed analysis from McMahon and/or their additional Jackson Hole experts. Ruth's own report admits that Rob Higbee applied the brakes approximately 1.4 seconds before the first impact. At least that shows Rob did not accelerate into the intersection as the Taylors had claimed. Moreover Ruth recognized Rob's reaction time was better than average, since he hit the brakes within one second of his first being able to see the van coming from his right. McMahon's report showed neither driver would have had a clear sight line of the other 2.2 seconds before the crash. But Ruth also speculates: "the braking prior to impact is not maximum braking; it averages about two-thirds of the maximum possible braking."

All of the experts I consulted told me the Ford device couldn't measure braking pressure; the only signal recorded is the "brake light" going on and off, not how hard the driver's foot is on the pedal. Even worse, Ruth injects into his report: "The vehicle EDR readout is consistent with the operator deciding to maintain speed and to not stop for the stop sign at the intersection." In other words, Ruth tried to manipulate the data he had from the box and suggest Rob Higbee should have seen the stop sign at 320 feet out and should have slammed on the brakes immediately. By not doing that, Ruth wanted to tell a jury that Rob must have decided not to stop, in order to help the prosecutor's criminal case. Now I knew what the prosecutor was going to try to do. By using Ruth's flawed conclusions, he wanted to supply some reason for the jury to conclude that Higbee decided to run the stop sign. We knew Higbee had no such intent, and had to get real experts to testify why this was an honest mistake in perception, not a criminal act.

For the rest of 2008 we used retired police officers as our volunteer investigators. John Heenan, retired from Atlantic City Police, and for years detailed to an FBI Strike Force, provided valuable insights for potential cross-examination of the state's witnesses. Thanks to the help of a traffic specialist in Ocean City, Manny Ridgeway and I went to the offices of the County Engineer, Dale Foster, to gather all of the material we could on the crucial intersection changes. We met frequently for hours on end at my house, always with Rob Higbee. With the help of a high-level law enforcement friend, I found Bruce Siddle, a police expert in the Midwest who had written and lectured extensively on "critical incidents" for law enforcement all over the world.

I also knew I needed a psychologist to explain Higbee's perception, reaction, inability to accurately remember all of the seconds before the crash, and to explain what really happened. We needed qualified experts to counter the prosecution's reliance on Richard Ruth.

Trial lawyers I know tell this story about F. Lee Bailey, a famous criminal defense attorney. As the story goes, Bailey was asked to give advice for success to a group of aspiring young advocates. When it came time for his speech, he stood up and said, "Preparation" and sat down. We had to prepare our case completely.

By the beginning of 2009, the STFA had spent much more on Rob's legal defense than ordinarily allowed, but this was different. "There but for the grace of God," thought many of the state police of all ranks. So the STFA, and even the unions of higher officers (NCO and superior officers) all pitched in to help Rob. More funds were raised somehow. Financial help from Police Benevolent Association (PBA), Fraternal Order of Police (FOP) groups, and individuals at various fundraisers enabled us to hire some expert witnesses. In preparing for trial, however, we had to be extremely careful how we used our limited resources.

Early on we decided that it was very likely the judge would allow data from the Ford EDR, since other courts involving other automobile brands had accepted its general theory as scientifically reliable. So instead of trying to hire our own EDR expert, we focused on how to use the state's data to our advantage. Perhaps we could limit Ruth's ability to give opinions beyond his expertise. We knew the prosecutor wanted to rely upon Ruth to persuade the jury that he could determine with numbers and measurements when Rob should have seen the stop sign.

Ruth thought he could say how hard and when Higbee should have applied his brakes to avoid the collision. But that all assumed Higbee knew the exact location of the stop sign and decided to ignore it. In January 2009, Richard Ruth was required to testify before the trial ever began. The judge had to rule in advance whether the EDR and Ruth's testimony would be admissible evidence when the jury trial began. As predicted, he found the EDR reliable scientific evidence. But we had requested and received Ruth's own notes from the quick "Human Factors" seminar that he took in June 2008. We were prepared to use them against him if the court decided to let him give opinions, beyond explaining what the downloaded numbers meant. After two days of testimony, the judge said that Ruth could testify about what he found from the so-called black box based upon his engineering expertise and experience at Ford. However, Judge Batten decided to throw out Ruth's opinions about accident reconstruction and what Ruth thought Higbee should have seen or done at certain pre-impact points. That was clearly a correct ruling by the judge and a major victory for us. Ruth simply was not qualified in those areas, but we needed experts who were.

There was another issue we thought the prosecutor would bring up to try to influence the jury against Trooper Higbee. Even though he never officially charged Higbee with lying, Meyer implied Higbee lied about stopping at the stop sign before going through the intersection. We knew Higbee had said he could not completely recall what happened in his October 2006 statement. But we needed to explain what happened to Rob's memory in this critical incident. Bruce Siddle, the police shooting expert, was going to help us with "critical incident amnesia."

We also located Professor Geoffrey Loftus, Chair of the Psychology Department at the University of Washington to help us explain what happens to memory in this type of traumatic event. We knew Rob was trying, but was unable to recall what actually happened seconds before the crash. We secretly had both Siddle and Loftus fly in separately to each view the scene, months before the trial was to begin. They had to formulate their own opinions based upon individual observations and after studying everything we obtained from the State.

I found Professor Loftus after talking with a Dartmouth classmate, a former Assistant United States Attorney who practices law in Washington, D.C. Roger Adelman prosecuted John Hinckley, Jr., who tried to assassinate President Reagan and asserted insanity as his defense. Adelman knew of experts in psychiatry and psychology across the country. When I spoke with Professor Loftus he seemed intrigued with the issues. When he reviewed all of the discovery materials we sent him he was shocked that the trooper had even been charged with a crime.

Professor Loftus was so incensed that the criminal charges were pending after reading everything, that he flew east from Seattle. He asked only for a minimal retainer and plane fare. He took the red-eye and we picked him up at the Newark Airport, driving straight down to the scene of the accident. He insisted on seeing everything in the darkness similar to the dark September night of the accident. He insisted on being driven back and forth, over and over, so he could see for himself the positioning of the stop signs and roadway. He had reviewed everything we had about the approach Rob would have seen. Because of his busy schedule, he wanted to meet with Rob and our investigative team to absorb everything.

We all worked straight through the night, finishing in the early morning at a diner for breakfast before taking Professor Loftus for his flight back west. We were exhausted, but he was convinced Sgt. McMahon's observations were correct. Rob would not have been able to see the stop sign and avoid the accident given the speed of both vehicles and the intersection's configuration. Moreover, he had an explanation for Rob's "faulty memory" based upon valid scientific experiments over the years. One more expert was needed to counter the prosecution case. Judge Alvarez ruled over my objection early in the case that the trooper could be judged on what a "reasonable law enforcement officer" would do under the circumstances, not just a "reasonable person."

We had to turn that ruling around to our advantage. I was determined to help the jury understand that is just what Rob did, even though he made an honest mistake. STFA President Davy Jones put me in touch with Frank Rodgers, who recently had retired as Lt. Col. (second in command) of the New Jersey State Police. I met him for a few hours for a long lunch in Ocean County. He agreed to review the materials and examine every state police protocol and standard operating procedure that might be relevant to evaluate Trooper Higbee's conduct that night.

Finally, after we received all three expert reports and shared them with our adversary, we thought we were almost prepared for the trial, now set for April 20, 2009. However, we did not anticipate the many pitfalls still in our path.

* * *

"Live free or die." I could not help thinking of the motto of New Hampshire, where I went to Dartmouth College, on many of those times I woke up at about three in the morning to rethink what more I should be doing to prevent Rob Higbee from going to prison. At the last pre-trial conference before moving forward to trial, Judge Batten asked that First Assistant Prosecutor Meyer and I confer to see if there was any last opportunity to reach any compromise to avoid trial. Up to now Rob faced a potential of ten years on each of the two counts of vehicular homicide, a second-degree felony. The judge would have discretion to make the sentences run concurrently, instead of consecutively. But Higbee would not be eligible for parole in less than eight years. Previously the prosecutor said he would recommend a four-year imprisonment.

At this last conference before trial, I was astonished that Meyer actually suggested he would recommend one year in jail if Rob would resign from the state police. Rob would also forfeit any opportunity to work in any public employment in New Jersey forever. My lawyer's ethical obligation required me to tell Rob of the offer. I took Rob aside in a small conference room just to the left of Judge Batten's courtroom.

When I told him, this gentle giant of a man looked down at me and said: "Bill, I have complete confidence in you. I know I will be found innocent and will not have to do one day in jail." No heavier burden can be put on a defense attorney than knowing the fate of an innocent man rests in your hands. We rejected the plea offer and the final stages of trial preparation were underway. It was all or nothing now; if found guilty, the risk was twenty years in prison.

We went back to trial preparation immediately. Investigator Manny Ridgeway and I had earlier talked with the speeder, young Josh Wigglesworth, with his parents present in their lawyer's office. We felt he would come forward and truthfully testify for us even if the prosecutor chose not to call him. He was scared of what might happen to him, but he knew he had to be accountable because his actions caused the trooper to follow him that fateful night. We also thought we had all of the engineering and intersection information ready to go into evidence.

We notified the judge and prosecutor months in advance that we intended to call County Engineer Dale Foster and his staff to explain the stop sign and overhead blinking light changes to the dangerous intersection. Because we still thought last minute legal issues might erupt during the trial, the STFA struck a deal with my former law firm and hired Donna Lee Vitale, an associate who had diligently worked on the case with me. She was to sit second chair at counsel table in the court and would have all of the hundreds of trial exhibits ready while I was on my feet during the trial. She would work all night if necessary if we needed a brief for the judge on short notice. She is attractive, but low key in the courtroom, and her presence might offset my sometimes-aggressive posture during trial. We could not afford the cost of professionals so we assembled a group of individuals we knew from all over Cape May County as a poor-man's jury consultant team to guess at jurors whom we would challenge. We did not want jurors who had any grudge against law enforcement.

We also worked for months to prepare suggested *voir dire* questions, for prospective jurors, to enable us to review their answers to see if they were biased against our client. Both the prosecutor and I shared lists of witnesses and exhibits to be introduced at trial to try to eliminate any surprises. We also were told that *TruTV* (formerly *Court TV*) was going to broadcast the trial live within guidelines and restrictions imposed by the court. The jurors could not be shown or identified by name on television, but otherwise the entire public record would be seen nationwide as it happened.

Provisions were made so that side bar conferences between the attorneys and the judge would not be heard. Jean Casarez, the on scene reporter, and her producer, Nancy Leung, requested that I give them all of the previous legal briefs by both sides and the court rulings so they could be fully prepared for the trial. Likewise the local reporter for *The Press of Atlantic City*, Trudi Gilfillian, seemed to make efforts to report both prosecution and defence positions, unlike the preconceived agenda we had seen with the *20/20* broadcast.

Even so, I had to simply take a calculated risk that we could obtain a fair and impartial jury in Cape May County, given the intense, pervasive, and often-adverse publicity Trooper Higbee had endured there. Though we did not move for a change of venue from Cape May County, several questions arose. Could we really find twelve people who could put aside emotions and sympathy for the tragic deaths of these two sisters? Would they be able to evaluate the mass of documentary evidence they would be given, and focus only on Rob Higbee's innocent state of mind? The reality of a criminal trial is that most people think a defendant must have done something criminal or the grand jury would not have returned an indictment. In this case, we now needed people on the jury who were sophisticated enough to afford Rob Higbee a real presumption of innocence throughout the trial.

Chapter 7

A defendant in a criminal trial should have a lot more control over who decides his fate. But, no defendant can choose a jury of his peers. It does not happen. All you can do is try to eliminate those with obvious bias against you, or who are totally incompetent to sit as jurors. Before the trial, both sides agreed with the judge that the defense could exercise twenty peremptory challenges to the prosecutor's twelve. That means each side has the right to strike a potential juror from the panel for no reason up to the number allotted. If the judge removed a potential juror for cause, that would not count against the number of peremptories.

The largely volunteer trial team pored over the jury lists every night as soon as we got them from the jury manager. The lists showed only: name, occupation, and town within Cape May County. The written answers filled out by each juror were given to both sides the night before the group would appear in court. We prepared criteria for evaluating each juror, hoping to eliminate criminal types or those with obvious bias against police. We needed intelligent jurors who could resist deciding the case based upon an outpouring of emotion for the tragic loss of the two young girls.

In part because of the high profile nature of the case, Judge Batten made significant rulings early on. Television coverage in the courtroom was to be as unobtrusive as possible and never show the faces of the jurors. Real court reporters as opposed to recordings would provide the record of the trial in case there was an appeal. I was provided with a real time monitor on my counsel table so I could read the testimony because of my hearing impairment. Finally, in a significant move,

Judge Batten allowed each counsel to ask questions of individual prospective jurors, without the rest of the group present. This procedure took longer but was much fairer to both sides. Days turned into weeks as each side made objections. The prosecutor did not want police or their relatives on the jury. We were concerned about persons who went to school or church with the victims or their family. Sometimes we had to use up our challenges to eliminate prospective panelists who knew or worked with family members.

Fortunately the judge let us extensively question those for whom we had real concern. Removed for cause by the judge were those with relatives in the state police who thought Rob should not have been indicted, but one man who did not know anyone in the case lived near the Woodbine state police barracks. He claimed: "all them troopers come whizzing past my house for no reason." He said they raced by his house at "120 miles per hour" all the time. At first the judge would not excuse him, because he did not know my client personally. But Rob worked out of that same barracks. With more questions, I finally got the person to admit that he'd read every single newspaper article and heard every program about the case. When it was apparent he had a bias against police, the court removed him for cause.

One potential juror declared she would be a basket case if she had to decide the matter. She was gone. A volunteer firefighter thought Higbee should have had red lights and siren on all the time and, therefore, was probably guilty. He was removed. Any juror who admitted to being even remotely familiar with the intersection was eliminated. One man was quickly removed when he told the judge the intersection was dangerous before the county put up the new blinking lights. The rest of the jurors did not hear this comment and were constantly warned by the judge not to go near the scene of the accident or they would be removed.

Even so, we still had to guess at whether a person might harbor a grudge against troopers. Maybe the juror got a traffic ticket or was treated badly by some cop once, and now was the chance to get even. We really could not know what was going on inside people's minds. One possible panelist said a police officer was less likely to tell the truth because he knew how to manipulate the system. He was not eliminated, but not ultimately chosen. Yet another said the opposite, knowing police would be disciplined for disregarding the truth. We lost that juror. Even casual acquaintances of some of Rob's potential character witnesses were eliminated for cause, yet some whose children had gone to school with the victims were allowed. A co-worker of the victim's grandfather could stay on the panel, as could a person who told the judge she had been broadsided in an accident. I objected, but the judge refused to remove her for cause.

The judge also recognized the influence of the Internet and tried to find out if anyone had visited any of the numerous websites concerning this case. He prohibited any deputy sheriff in his courtroom who had visited such an Internet site. We found out there had been over three-thousand hits on a site supporting the trooper and just under a hundred against him at that time. The court also made sure none of the jurors would know that the State of New Jersey had settled the civil suit by the family against the state police for two million dollars before the trial.

We had to prove to the court actual bias to remove a juror for cause because almost everyone in the potential panel had read or heard something about the case. We knew we might have to use up some of our precious peremptory challenges to prevent someone with a predisposition against Rob. Midway through the selection, Judge Batten almost reversed himself and was contemplating lowering the number of our challenges to speed up the process. After I exclaimed he could not change the rules in the middle of the game, and even the prosecutor agreed, the judge relented and kept the original number of challenges. Still, the stress of trying to figure out who would decide Rob's fate remained largely guess work, intuition, and reading body language by our support group in the courtroom, including Rob's wife Beth, and my wife, Petie. Their insights watching people were invaluable. With help from Burgos, Vitale, Ridgeway, and Rob himself, we made lists in order, worst to best, so I could strike those we disliked the most.

The prosecutor wanted to get into evidence some gruesome photos of the victims after the accident, so the judge inquired in advance if any juror would have a problem viewing them. One person said she would have difficulty looking at them because she sat behind the family in church, but she vowed to "do my best." She was not removed for cause even though she was asked about preconceived notions and responded: "I hope not, but I know the results of the civil trial through a newspaper account, and I know the grand jury called for a criminal trial." She did not make the final panel of jurors.

Two and a half weeks had gone by before we arrived at sixteen jurors (twelve plus four alternates, to be removed from the panel at random at the end of the trial). The big challenge for our side was to be sure that they knew the difference between civil responsibility for an *accident* and proof *beyond a reasonable doubt* that a *crime* took place.

Jury selection is "an inexact art at best," intoned a weary Judge Batten, after eleven days in the courtroom so far. Finally the diverse group of nine men and seven women (twelve plus alternates) assembled in the jury box and rose to take their oaths on May 6, 2009. They swore to fairly and truly decide the facts in the dispute between the State of New Jersey and Rob Higbee, as to the vehicular homicide charges against him. They sat in their seats as they had been randomly selected, after others had been removed by the judge or by request of one of the attorneys. We knew the lady formerly in business in seat number one would be the forelady by court rule.

I had been convinced by Rob's observations that she was a mature intelligent woman whose attitude indicated she could objectively sift through the facts. I mused to myself about what I needed to convince each of them. The artist with a background in sales would need a clear picture of what happened. The union steam fitter I thought would be able to be fair because he had police officer relatives. The retired postmaster had to be familiar with the area in Marmora, even though he supervised in Cape May Court House. The retired military officer and the ironworker could understand split-second decisions in precarious situations. The veterinary assistant had seen many police K-9 officers in doctor's office practice, so again I hoped for fairness.

Several of the jurors were from Ocean City where the victims had gone to school, but they seemed to be able to put emotions aside. The nurse could readily understand the effects of the concussion and traumatic accident on Rob's memory, as perhaps would the physical therapist. The truck driver and the technician, who worked for a communications provider, might be vaguely familiar with the intersection, but I needed to have them picture what it was like at night. The former Motor Vehicle investigator had seen many accident scenes so this one had to be explained in detail. An Ocean City secretary worked for Public Works. She had many contacts with local police, and she appeared to be unbiased. I counted on the careful expertise of the aeronautics engineer and the surveyor/civil engineer to understand the crucial details of data and measurements, which would show the difficulty of perception for Rob, approaching the intersection.

Crammed into the rest of the day after the jury was sworn in, were preliminary instructions by the judge, and the opening statements by both counsel. I had sat in the courtroom watching Dave Meyer in other criminal cases, so I had some idea of what to expect. I avoided use of the same blue and yellow power point he normally used. But I knew I had to counter his graphic illustrations on the prosecutor's permanent flat screen on the wall right over the jury. My slides had to be projected on the blank wall far away from the jury. I hoped they could see what my volunteers helped me to prepare. I can't speak for Meyer, but I had tossed around possible opening remarks in my mind for more than two years now.

David Meyer opened to the jury at about 3:25 p.m. He showed an illuminated stop sign on the screen. He read words taken from the defendant's statement three weeks after the occurrence: "as I approached the intersection, I remember stopping and looking both ways and proceeding through the intersection."

Meyer retorted, "if only that were so," suggesting we would not be here, and the Becker family would be looking forward to celebrating Mother's Day this Sunday. Meyer never read the rest of Higbee's interview when the trooper revealed "blankness" in his memory and the uncertainty of his recollections. In a further attempt to project Higbee as attempting to lie about stopping, Meyer suggested that the entire state police were not even aware of the Event Data Recorder in the Ford Crown Victoria at the time of the statement in October 2006.

We knew that was not true. Meyer explained his version of the law to the jury. He had to prove Higbee was driving; and "but for" his actions the girls would not have died. Meyer said Higbee was "reckless." That meant Rob "consciously disregarded a substantial and unjustifiable risk" resulting in causing death or serious bodily harm. We knew that should be the point of focus: Higbee's state of mind.

Meyer produced charts in his power point that Ruth had prepared for him. He was attempting to use the PCM data to prove Higbee was reckless. He contended Higbee sped up as he neared the intersection. "The car he was endeavoring to close the gap with was some distance ahead and he just blew into the intersection." He argued once Higbee saw the "…stop sign ahead, his foot hovered over that brake pedal, but not applying it with any significant force…" Meyer showed aerial views of the scene, and admitted Higbee made "contact with the brake pedal" just before the impact, but could not possibly have stopped and looked both ways. Therefore, he argued because Higbee did not "…meaningfully slow down, did not hit his brakes hard enough and soon enough, he must have knowingly disregarded the stop sign."

Meyer told the jury it was understandable that the girls may have been traveling in the mid-forties above the 35 mph zone because that is what we all recognize as "routine traffic patterns." But he said the trooper, although permitted to exceed the limit to catch a speeder was not justified here in a "pursuit" at "almost twice the speed limit" without red lights and siren. He confused the jury into thinking this was an illegal "pursuit." The times the brakes were applied he characterized as "coasting" not "hard braking."

Meyer made the same argument to the jury as he had told Wythe and me in his office before the indictment. Higbee should have known exactly where the stop sign was since he had seen the reverse gray side of the sign as he turned into Stagecoach Road earlier. He further told the jury to disregard any evidence of intervening causation by the passenger not having her seatbelt on. He also suggested that the configuration of the intersection was likewise irrelevant in their deliberations. He told them not to consider "any contributory defect with the intersection itself."

Meyer claimed the defendant disregarded state police SOP's and AG Guidelines in failing to cautiously proceed through the intersection after stopping. That assumes Higbee actually was aware of the location of the stop sign. In explaining why this was a criminal case Meyer conceded Higbee did not mean to kill the girls, and it was not an attack on his character. "It's the criminal act that's punished, not the person." He continued: "Sometimes good people do bad things. This is just such an instance."

Then he went on to exonerate the young speeder Josh Wigglesworth by saying he properly waited to be pulled over at some point by the trooper, but bore no responsibility for the inappropriate response of "the defendant" (Higbee) to the speeder's violation. He also failed to mention Wigglesworth never pulled over when he saw the trooper. Meyer told the jury: "What happened here was not a mistake by a reasonable law enforcement officer. What happened here was a gross error beyond that which any reasonable law enforcement officer could suggest was appropriate under these circumstances." The prosecutor told the jury that at the end of the case they would find that the defendant caused the deaths recklessly and consequently Higbee would be guilty of the crime of vehicular homicide.

My turn. "This was a tragic accident—not a crime." This criminal trial was not about the horrendous results of a crash. The jury must decide the fate of Rob Higbee based upon his state of mind before the accident. The prosecutor just conceded "the defendant" did not mean to kill the girls. But if he could convince the jury that he was "reckless" then Rob would be found guilty.

I had rehearsed my opening in my mind hundreds of times, while riding my bicycle on the Boardwalk, while rowing my single scull in the back bay, while tossing and turning at night, and while sitting and watching Rob during our many times together. An opening is supposed to be an outline of your case. But often the defense has to answer the prosecutor's case and we can't always predict what will be presented. I am always very guarded in specifics because someone on the jury will always pick up on something you promise, but don't deliver by the end of the trial, so I focused on the facts I expected to bring out. I spoke only about the law as I was sure would be a part of the judge's charge to the jury as the attorneys had discussed with him.

It was 4:34 p.m. when Meyer finished his opening to the jury. I had to cut my remarks down. The jury normally sat until 4:00 or 4:30. The judge indicated both counsel should address the jury the same day and asked the panel to stay longer tonight. The jury was briefly excused. I approached the judge with Mr. Meyer at sidebar. I told Judge Batten the victims' mother appeared to be seen by at least two jurors noticeably sobbing in the court. The judge asked Meyer to do his best to speak with her to avoid distractions, but she obviously had a right to be there at all times during the trial if she chose. The jury was due back from the precise ten-minute recess.

I needed to defend my client. In almost every case I have tried over the years, I have kept strict control over my emotions, but this was the most difficult challenge I have had as an advocate. A friend and neighbor with whom I had practiced law, Gino Santori, had left me a note the night before. He told me this one was different and it is okay for the jury to see your passion to protect Rob. As a former prosecutor, Gino also realized what this case meant to police everywhere. I knew protecting Trooper Rob Higbee's innocence was up to me now. My wife, Petie, sat a few rows behind me. She reminded me I needed to put my notes aside and look at each juror in the eye as I spoke.

I walked over to the jury box and I began to tell the jurors about Rob Higbee as a person and as a trooper, not as a "defendant." Unlike most of us, his duty required him to perform functions that involve risks. He was charged with enforcing the law. He cannot ignore violations. The speeder might be an escaped felon, a rapist, or a terrorist. The trooper cannot know who the suspect is until he closes the gap and sees the license plate and possibly the driver. All Rob saw was a dark colored vehicle doing 65 mph in a 35 mph zone on a dark road at night. It was not a "pursuit" yet. He wasn't close enough to turn on emergency lights and pull over the speeder.

Meyer had tried to minimize for the jury the confusing and dangerous intersection as a factor in the accident. But I had to tell them what the scene looked like to Rob. That was crucial to our defense.

The Jurors needed to know about the poor sight lines, the obstructions, the lack of lighting, and the speeder's headlights on the stop sign at the next intersection ahead, not the one Rob was approaching. I told the jury that the stop sign at Stagecoach and Tuckahoe Roads "is further right than normal." I quoted those words directly from Sgt. McMahon's expert report to the prosecutor. I knew that was in the State's case, so it had to come out during the testimony. That was important to show how hard it was to see that sign at Stagecoach Road with peripheral vision at night.

Of course, Rob Higbee would have slowed down and stopped had he known where the stop sign was. I implored the jury to apply good common sense. I asked: "Ladies and gentlemen, why would any individual, let alone a trained state trooper ignore the risk to himself and others and decide to go through a stop sign?" Meyer had told the jury Higbee was dazed, but aware of his surroundings, implying he should have complete recall. Higbee had tried his best to explain what he remembered. Obviously his intent was always to stop and look before going through an intersection. But when, if ever, did he know he was crossing Tuckahoe Road before the impact?

I fumbled through my power point presentation projected on the wall (see pages 137-142). I realized the time in the courtroom was almost 5:30. I had to end quickly. As I explained the presumption of innocence, I asked the jurors to look over at Rob Higbee, and pledge that they would maintain that presumption in his favor throughout the trial. It was the prosecutor's burden to prove a criminal reckless state of mind. If the prosecutor cannot prove that, Rob Higbee is still innocent. I know my voice cracked, as I looked over at Rob and said to the Jury: "We are here because this case is about him. You are going to decide his fate. Our fate is in your hands. You are going to decide whether he committed a crime." I said that if the state did not prove each and every element beyond a reasonable doubt, he was still innocent.

The judge excused the jury at 5:32 p.m. and told them to be back for the first witness at 9:00 a.m. the next day. The openings by counsel were over. Finally, the jury would hear and see whether the prosecutor really had any evidence to support the charges against Rob Higbee.

Chapter 8

No wound cuts as deep into the soul as the loss of a child. My own brother lost a son to a deranged killer. I decided that there was no way that I would attempt to cross-examine the state's first witness, Caesar Caiafa. The grieving grandfather described the victims as if they were his daughters. They frequently stayed with Caesar and his wife instead of with their own mother. He tearfully described searching for his missing van that terrible night. "I had a gut feeling my children were involved in the accident," he said.

His anguish spilled over into frustration with the state police for not letting him near the accident scene for hours to find out if those were "his girls." I chose to end the emotional agony of his direct examination by rising and saying, "No questions, Your Honor." The prosecutor's case moved forward with tedious and graphic testimony, visual footage of the highly illuminated crime scene that night, and aerial views of the intersection, which made it seem so clearly defined, from high above the ground.

At a break in the testimony, one of the jurors, a land surveyor, asked to speak with the attorneys and the judge outside of the presence of the rest of the panel. He told the judge that with his background, he had seen something in the overhead photos that perhaps the others had not. The court correctly instructed him that he was free to indicate his comments to the panel like everyone else, as long as he did not suggest his expertise was superior to any other juror's evaluation of the facts. He was told not to discuss the case with anyone until the jury deliberated at the end of the trial. I remained optimistic from this juror's remarks, but I could not know if his observations were beneficial to us or to the prosecution. Before the next witness was to testify, the judge informed us without the jury, that he had made another tentative legal ruling. Judge Batten stated that, in an effort to preserve an even playing field, he would preclude any references to prior accidents at the intersection and would allow no information about any subsequent remedial changes to it. He implied we could still supply additional briefs on the subject, but I thought quickly to myself that the ruling had completely undermined my theory of the defense.

The prosecution continued with Karen Giblin, a wispy plain woman who lived near the scene and worked at the pharmacy in the Wayside Village Shops. On September 27, 2006 she heard what, "sounded like speeding past my house" on Stagecoach Road, just south of Tuckahoe Road. "Where I live a lot of people go fast," and she said she remembered previous accidents there. She heard a "crash" and then "silence." She called 911. Giblin admitted she did not see the accident take place. When she ran from her house to the intersection she saw a man who pointed up the road in the direction of a van and said, "Don't go there."

On cross-examination she was unable to identify the reverse side of the crucial stop sign in the photo the prosecutor had previously shown to her. It was not visible and she was not sure of its location, even though she lived near there for about ten years. How would the trooper be expected to have noticed it and remembered the sign after turning south that night? That was a question I hoped the jury would later ask themselves. Giblin heard other speeders over the years, but had never called the police before. She agreed there were no blinking lights over the intersection at the time of the accident. Because of the ruling of the judge, I stopped my questions there.

Anthony Cinaglia and his friend, Melissa Lipstein, were the next witnesses. By chance before the trial, my investigator Manny Ridgeway, the ex-state police detective, had come across Cinaglia while walking on the Ocean City Boardwalk and struck up a conversation. Cinaglia volunteered to him that Prosecutor Meyer was most anxious to have Cinaglia testify to the "flash of a speeding car" to attempt to prove Higbee accelerated into the intersection. Cinaglia told Ridgeway he would tell the truth, but he said he told Meyer if you want me to help convict the trooper, "I'm not your man." With that in mind, I was very careful on cross. Cinaglia testified he heard nothing before the collision itself and never saw the girls' van before the impact. He did not speculate that the trooper accelerated into the intersection. He called 911 from Melinda's cell phone. He described Higbee as "visibly shaken" and remembered the trooper telling him to check on the other drivers. The prosecutor sought to have Melinda describe the sound of a "whoosh" or "swoosh" before the accident. But on cross, I confronted her with her statement to the detectives. She admitted seeing a "flash," but told them nothing about any sounds before the accident. No acceleration. Maybe I had put some little dents into the prosecution's case.

Trooper John Schulke was obviously uncomfortable as he took the witness stand for the prosecution at the beginning of the fourth week of the Higbee trial. With the starched slate blue uniform and close crew cut, Schulke was every bit the professional, but he had worked with Rob and was conflicted. He was required to tell the truth, but was not allowed to tell the whole truth. On questioning by Prosecutor Meyer, Schulke related the first dispatch gave the intersection as Roosevelt, not Tuckahoe. He realized that was wrong and stated: "I knew exactly where the accident occurred because I was there at accidents previously." Neither prosecutor nor judge said anything about Schulke's comment. I believed that remark "opened the door" to my asking Schulke questions on cross-examination as to his knowledge of the previous accidents at the scene.

Schulke lived near the area and at one point in his answers to the prosecutor's questions, described it as a "bad intersection." The judge quickly intervened on his own and instructed the jury to disregard the adjective. When it was time for my cross, the court ruled specifically no mention could be made of any of the previous twenty-six accidents at the scene. At a sidebar, I reminded the judge, to no avail, that I had notified him and the prosecutor months in advance that I wanted to use that information. I had given Meyer, two years before the trial, material from the county engineer about the dangerous intersection. Still, the judge said unless I could prove the intersection was "illegal" according to some state or national highway transportation standard, that no evidence of its inadequate configuration would be admitted at the trial. This seemed to be an impossible task.

Schulke did help me clarify that the brightly illuminated photographs shown to the jury were really not representative of what it would like to a driver in the darkness. Furthermore, I was able to show Higbee was properly following NJSP protocols by closing the gap on the speeder without red lights and siren. Moreover, Schulke confirmed Higbee was only semi-conscious when he saw the trooper emerge from the patrol car. Rob was limping and had to lean on Schulke for support before he got him to an ambulance.

The next two witnesses were hardly objective or responsive and required treatment by me as clearly hostile. Robert Taylor and his son Michael had been sitting in their Mazda at the stop sign facing Higbee's approach. Robert Taylor was still seeking damages for his minor injuries in a pending civil suit against Higbee and the state police. Robert Taylor's high forehead reflected the courtroom lights. His demeanor reminded me of the cartoon character Elmer Fudd. He stared out at the prosecutor from wire-rimmed glasses.

Taylor was dressed in a white shirt, light blue tie, dark blue sport shirt, and khaki pants. He could not conceal his willingness to blurt out his story as quickly as possible, hardly waiting for the question to end before he jumped in with his answer. The father wanted to paint himself as a person with an impeccable memory as he related his trip home on a "deserted" Stagecoach Road that night. He did not notice any "speeder" in the opposite direction, although he described seeing a possum coming across the road looking over its shoulder at him as if to say, *What are you looking at?*

Taylor claimed that when he approached the intersection, his son called his attention to a white car coming at them "driving crazy." I objected to that characterization, not only because it was inadmissible "opinion" evidence, but also it was hearsay because he claimed his son said it, not him. The judge sustained my objection, but the jury had already heard the comment and it is very hard to "unring a bell" once you have already heard it. Taylor tried to suggest he knew it was a "police car" and that he never took his eyes off of it. He stated flatly: "I never saw a car blow a stop sign before."

Robert Taylor never saw the girls' Dodge van approaching his left. When the van impacted his Mazda he described it as a "...surprise, like closing a door, a pancake," and "...crushing metal and glass like a shotgun." He said there was glass all over him and the impact of the Becker vehicle was "...like a sledgehammer smashing us." He first talked of cuts above his right eye until he realized his mistake and explained it was his left eye and leg since the impact was on his driver's side. He complained it took a while for the emergency responders to help him. The prosecutor tried to suggest the word "sideswipe" in his question about the crash, but the judge agreed with me saying the characterization was "somewhat misleading."

When it was my turn to question, I knew I could not let him suggest to the jury that he saw the patrol car accelerate into the intersection. I confronted Taylor with his previous statements to the investigators shortly after the accident. He told them he heard the patrol car approaching, but did not actually see it. At the trial, Taylor exclaimed, "No, I saw it the whole time." He repeated quickly, "I saw the vehicle the whole time." I showed him the transcribed statement, which had been tape-recorded at the time. He called the crash "an explosion," but told the authorities at that time: "I never saw what hit me, it was a sliding metal mass."

At the police barracks he said he knew it was a police car when he spotted the insignia on the side of the patrol car after it stopped in the woods near his car. But at the trial he insisted his eyes never left the "speeding police car." What was his explanation for the inconsistency?

He said: "I suppose they didn't write it down correctly." I then read to him this exchange which was taped and transcribed when he spoke with the prosecutor's own representative and the state police detective: "Question: You did not notice any vehicle in front of you or down the street approaching that intersection prior to the impact? Answer: No." What was his explanation under oath at the trial? Taylor exclaimed: "It's fantasy! This is fantasy – this is something I never said. It is fantasy."

His outburst was a defense attorney's dream. The seasoned prosecutor was careful to show no emotion after hearing Taylor's remark. Taylor insisted at the trial he heard the trooper accelerate and his eyes were fixed on the patrol car even though he'd previously said all he knew was something "big and white" had hit his car. His memory was "crystal clear" at the trial despite what he had previously said.

I correctly anticipated Taylor's son Michael would mimic his father's incredible testimony and prepared accordingly for the next morning. Michael showed up with a swagger, dressed in jeans with his shirttail hanging out. He insisted he had not discussed the case with his father at home over the evening recess. Michael remembered the "muskrat" crossing the road, but, of course, did not see the "speeder." He then said he was sure his father had looked both right and left at the intersection. He could tell it was a police car coming at them, because, even though its headlights were directly in his eyes, he could see the police logo on the side of the door as the patrol car sped in their direction.

In his first statement to the investigators the day after the accident, Michael estimated that the police car was maybe 60 feet away when he first saw it. He also had told them it looked like "the police car was going to stop someone." He never noticed the Beckers' Dodge van before the impact. Michael had previously testified "the police car was coming very fast at us and it accelerated." He had admitted that the area was only dimly lit and that he neither saw nor heard the van. In an attempt to undermine his credibility, I then asked him how could he attribute the sound of "acceleration" to the police car. His response was that he was familiar with the sound of "trooper cars" on the Parkway and on the street because they make a distinct sound when they accelerate, that is when they "put pedal to the metal."

He repeated that phrase adding that's what happens when "police cars are in pursuit." I then asked Michael if he personally had ever been issued a traffic ticket by the police. The prosecutor objected to the question and the judge sustained the objection. I just hoped the jury would hear evidence later to show that Higbee had not accelerated into the intersection as the Taylors claimed, and that he had tried to stop his vehicle as soon as he perceived the danger.

Young Josh Wigglesworth appeared in sharp contrast to the Taylor witnesses. He looked like a scared jackrabbit as he took the stand that May 12 afternoon. Unlike the arrogant and opinionated Michael Taylor, Josh was hesitant and obviously uncomfortable. Slight of build and looking forlorn, he struggled to keep his composure as he attempted to relate what had happened that fateful night.

The prosecutor was wary and careful with Josh. He had known he would need to produce Josh as a witness or I would call him. I had Josh's sworn statement to Meyer's own investigator from October 2006 even though the public had not been told. Josh talked with us more than once before the trial. He was still afraid of what the prosecutor might do to him, but the passage of time made charges against Josh unlikely. Manny and I believed he would tell the truth no matter what the consequences.

Josh's testimony was objective. He did not volunteer some rehearsed opinion. He politely answered, "Yes, sir" or "No, sir" to both attorneys. He admitted he was the "speeder." He had been stopped before. He knew the routine. He didn't know the headlights from the opposite direction were from a cop until he passed them. Then he saw the lettering and the NJSP triangle on the side of the car. He looked down, flipped his full headlights on, and tried to slow down. But he kept going, even when he saw the police car make a K-turn and start after him. He would wait for the red lights when the cop got close enough to see his license and signal for him to pull over. Until then he could keep going. Maybe he would not catch up with him and he would go on home.

On cross, Josh admitted that he had lost sight of the trooper's headlights behind him, as he went down a slight dip in the road before Tuckahoe Road. I knew Rob would later say he lost sight of the speeder's taillights at that moment. Josh confirmed his headlights were on the stop sign at Roosevelt, the next intersection, as he saw the crash in his rear view mirror. I hoped the jury would later conclude that was the stop sign Rob Higbee mistakenly took to be the one at Tuckahoe Road. The day ended with an emergency responder admitting Higbee could have suffered a concussion from his head injuries. The paramedic admitted that might lead to amnesia. The jury would have to put these little pieces of the puzzle together later when they deliberated.

Sgt. Karl Ulbrich was the lead criminal investigator for the state police. Everything he did to gather the facts was coordinated with the prosecutor's detective, Lt. Eugene Taylor. When Prosecutor Robert Taylor gave the okay for Higbee to be indicted by the grand jury in February 2007, neither McMahon nor Ulbrich were even told. They both thought it was being considered an "accident." which is why the designation "A" still appeared on their reports.

The reason Meyer called Ulbrich at the trial, in my opinion, was he wanted to focus on the statement Higbee had given, to make it look like Higbee had lied during his interview. If the jury believed he had lied about "stopping and looking both ways" at the intersection, they might believe he deliberately went through the stop sign. Meyer would not call Lt. Eugene Taylor because of the inconsistencies in his grand jury testimony that I knew about.

When Karl Ulbrich appeared before the jury, he looked like a prizefighter dressed as an old style FBI Agent. He wore a white shirt, plain brown tie, and dark pinstriped suit. He spoke in succinct words, in an even monotone, removing any hint of emotion in the courtroom. In his thorough manner, he had eliminated any "personal or work related stressors" that could have had any impact on Rob Higbee before the accident.

He had also taken great care not to let Rob know of the rumors that he already had heard about a speeder before he first interviewed Higbee. He wanted to hear his version so he could check on its accuracy. He was able to find and talk with Wigglesworth about a week after Rob's interview. Moreover, he and McMahon were both able to recreate the movements of Higbee and Wigglesworth and believed they were consistent. Ulbrich was convinced he had found the speeder Higbee was attempting to catch that night.

Meyer brought out what he maintained were inconsistent remarks. Ulbrich stated Higbee told him: "He believed he stopped and looked both ways." But Ulbrich added Higbee said "...as best as he could remember" and not that he "remembered." Ulbrich was told of the order by the prosecutor to file motor vehicle charges against Higbee since they had to be served within thirty days of the incident. I wanted the jury to know Rob still faced some punishment for the accident even if he was acquitted of the criminal charges.

I speculated that Meyer wanted them to know of the "careless driving" ticket, because they might confuse that standard with "reckless" and think he was guilty of vehicular homicide.

I wanted to have the judge explain the difference to the jury at that point, but he declined, saying he would properly instruct them at the end of the trial. So it was before the jury without much clarity. On cross examination Ulbrich helped me explain the difference between "closing the gap" and a "pursuit." He said: "When a person is being followed by a trooper who cannot yet identify the driver and the license plate, and has no lights and sirens on, he continues until the trooper clearly indicates he wants to pull him over, that is, puts on his red lights and sirens. At that point if the suspect pulls over right away or at least within a reasonable distance at a safe stop, he has complied with the officer's orders and an investigation will be completed. If the violator chooses to speed off and disregard the red lights and sirens, it then becomes a 'pursuit.'"

Ulbrich described the differences between the two as being "violator driven." A violator eluding the police in a "pursuit" is "consciously disregarding" the officer's clear signal to pull over. I was very pleased he used the description "conscious disregard" because I wanted the jury to realize a person had to make a deliberate decision, not just a mistake in perception to commit a crime. That was the heart of the defense. A speeder would not be a criminal for "eluding" or "avoiding apprehension" unless he decided to escape. Rob would not be a criminal unless he "consciously disregarded," that is ignored, a stop sign.

I was able to have Ulbrich describe the attempt to recreate Higbee's approach to the scene. Ulbrich noted the stop sign at Tuckahoe appears "…further to the right than the stop sign at Roosevelt." The remark apparently went unnoticed by the prosecutor and the judge because no objection was made. But I knew I could later refer to it in my summation at the end of the case.

Finally, I needed to diffuse the impression that Higbee had lied. He had struggled with a faulty memory to explain why he went through the stop sign. I took a chance and asked Ulbrich: "Do you think Trooper Higbee in his statement was in any way attempting to deceive you?"

His answer: "I don't believe he was trying to be deceptive; however, what he said was inconsistent with what the dynamics of the crash were." Ulbrich did not think Higbee had lied. The lead detective had no part in bringing about the criminal indictment. But the prosecutor had decided Higbee was guilty of a crime.

Chapter 9

The mobile video recorder captured the emergency response of Shift Supervisor NJSP Sgt. Anthony Mertis at about 10:12 p.m. because the red lights and siren triggered the recording. Fire and Rescue crews were already there, along with other police. Floodlights and headlights brightly illuminated the scene. When Mertis testified for the state, the jury viewed the only nighttime picture of the stop sign as it then existed. Meyer showed the video and froze the frame with a blue halo around the stop sign from all of the lights, clearly not the way Rob Higbee would have seen it.

Much of the time outside of the jury's presence that fourth week of trial was spent in arguments to allow us to counter that visual representation. The prosecutor had failed to preserve the original stop sign and we were now told we could not use any of the photos or videos taken in the months after the incident because various improvements had been made. We were not permitted to show the jury any comparison between the old and new stop signs, or even mention how the lighting had been improved, let alone the new overhead blinking yellow and red lights at the intersection. I argued the prosecutor had failed to preserve "exculpatory evidence" by failing to preserve viable images and the original stop sign. The judge said we should have sought a court order back in 2006, even though we had no idea then Rob would ever be charged with a crime.

Frustrated at not being able to have a visual to show the jury, I even had a local artist friend, Carl L. Rosner, a retired illustrator, prepare artist renderings of what Higbee would have seen, based upon the testimony of the state's own witnesses (*see pages 143-145*). That too was rejected. The judge told us he had seen a computerized recreation of President Kennedy's assassination and suggested we should attempt to get a computerized version of our accident scene. We knew we could not afford that expense. I had been trying for two years to anticipate what I could show the jury. Now all of the detailed information from the county engineer was ruled inadmissible.

I had planned to call County Traffic Maintenance Supervisor Ron Hearon, to show the improvements. Instead, now Meyer proposed to call him to testify that the day after the accident Hearon was able to stand in the middle of Stagecoach Road and see the stop sign clearly without obstructions, 350 feet from the intersection. I practically screamed how unfair and misleading that would be. Meyer was also going to have Hearon produce some reflective surface Hearon had made in his shop to show how bright the stop sign would be when light was on it. I finally convinced the judge to preclude all opinion evidence by this proposed witness as unreliable because the employee admitted he was colorblind.

Our trial team spent the entire weekend in a valiant effort to develop some acceptable illustration for the jury. With the help of former police friends of Davy Jones and the STFA, we went back again to the scene. David Liske and Pete Scalia, of Liske Forensic Engineers, Inc. from upstate New York, came down to Cape May on short notice and tried everything they could to reproduce the scene and demonstrate the changes, but those photos (*see page 150*) were not admitted at the trial.

Their problems were insurmountable. They would have to replace the new stop signs, remove the overhead blinking lights, and reposition the permanent street light which now shined toward the stop sign. They took enhanced night photos. Even after the improvements, the approach was still hidden by the many utility poles in front of the sign, but now you could spot the intersection a mile away because you could see the overhead red blinker light, which would have prevented this horrible accident. There was simply nothing we could do to show the jury what Rob would have seen that night in the darkness just before the crash.

We might be limited to a verbal description based upon Sgt. McMahon's attempt to retrace Rob's route the night after the incident. The pressure on all of us was enormous. Would the jury be able to picture what really happened when the photos Meyer showed them were taken in daylight from the middle of the road where the stop sign was clearly visible? This case had implications looming for all of law enforcement.

We received communications from across the country, concerned about the fate of the trooper. A police officer from Cleveland said his whole shift was watching the trial on TV and they worried that honest mistakes might lead to jail. A local deputy fire chief told me he had reprimanded a young firefighter for delay in responding to a working fire. The firefighter had been following the Higbee case on TV, and told his superior officer: "I am not going to jail just to do my job and get to the fire. No one will apparently protect us from prosecution, so why should I take that risk?" How could we tell the jury about this dilemma for every emergency responder?

Richard Ruth, the ex-Ford engineer, traveled to the trial from Michigan. As a proposed expert, he first had to satisfy the judge on direct and cross before the jury could hear his opinion. I was able to show Ruth had made mistakes in his own recollection of when and where he had previously testified, even a few months before.

At one point Ruth quipped in answering me, "You gave me a memory test and I failed the memory test." He tried to minimize his inaccurate previous testimony before the same judge back in the hearing in January. He maintained his testimony in another state helped to convict another defendant. However, he later admitted he never testified at any trial, but simply briefed a proposed state's witness.

Ruth was determined to portray himself as a qualified expert in interpreting the data downloaded from the PCM in the 2005 Ford Crown Victoria driven by Trooper Higbee the night of the fatalities. But it seemed obvious to me that he also wanted to put his own spin on the numbers to embellish his presentation for the prosecution. He could not claim expertise in human factors, but he still wanted to manipulate his interpretation of the figures. The prosecutor wanted Ruth to imply that Rob was reckless and contended he did not hit the brakes soon enough or hard enough to avoid the collision. How did he propose to show that?

Conveniently, Ruth had left Ford and with some colleagues had conducted an experiment on the exact same type of 2005 Ford model "police package" up in Ontario, Canada. However, Ruth had been in the passenger seat when the experiment was conducted. It was on an unobstructed test area in daylight, instead of the darkened conditions our trooper had faced. But most importantly, Ruth had told the test drivers in advance that they would be expected to hit the brakes as hard as they could upon a signal. Therefore, they could anticipate maximum braking upon command. Rob, on the other hand, had not known precisely where the stop sign was and had no idea he would be encountering a vehicle speeding toward him from his right until 2.2 seconds before the crash.

Ruth was permitted to discuss his findings to illustrate his conclusion Rob Higbee did not hit the brakes with maximum pressure before he would have seen the girls' van. Ruth compared stopping distances with his arranged experiment to argue how hard he thought Higbee should have applied the brakes. I objected in the course of this testimony because the measurement of the brake pedal can show only "on" and "off" when the brake light is activated. It does not measure the degree of pressure applied by the driver's foot. Ruth wanted to have the jury believe there was only "small" pressure on the brake pedal at the time Higbee should have seen the stop sign in his approach. The judge sustained that objection, but later permitted Ruth to substitute the word "slight."

Ruth also wanted to categorize about 300 feet before the impact as the "decision point" because that is where he concluded a driver would have had to apply the brakes once he saw the stop sign, to avoid the crash. The stop sign is approximately 50 feet before the impact. Therefore, the brakes had to be applied 250 feet before the stop sign. The real problem with that logic is how can you assume precisely where Rob ever saw the Tuckahoe Road stop sign at night while closing the gap? The jury was told to disregard "decision point," but still was left to speculate as to when Rob could have seen the stop sign and should have braked accordingly.

The charts prepared by Ruth for the jury to see were also misleading. He kept referring on the charts to a "pursuit" when it was "closing the gap," according to the prosecutor's own state police witnesses. The judge left the words on the chart, deciding the jury could sort it out with proper instructions. To my advantage, his charts also showed Higbee's speed as low as 62 miles per hour at several points. Contrary to that fact, Lt. Eugene Taylor had testified before the grand jury that Higbee's speed never dropped below 70 miles per hour. But the prosecution at trial never called the lieutenant of county detectives, so this jury would not know of that discrepancy, even though it was part of the testimony used to secure the indictment against Higbee. Ruth also tried to say Higbee's foot was "hovering over the brake pedal" as he would have passed the "stop ahead" sign. I wanted the jury to know the misrepresentation. The foot had to be either "on" or "off" to trigger the brake light. I needed the jury to understand that this was not objective evidence to conclude what was in Higbee's mind.

Ruth also had to admit to a margin of error in all of his calculations. He "assumed" an average of 60 miles per hour, or 100 feet per second. The data recorder is only accurate to .2 seconds. Therefore, there could have been a 20-foot error based upon every .2 seconds in his recorded information. In addition, Ruth only approximated the point of impact and distances by pacing off distances himself instead of using a precise measuring device when he visited the scene years after the accident.

Eventually, we were able to show that it was just as reasonable to conclude that Higbee might have started applying the brakes as soon as he saw the "Stop Ahead" sign. He had to locate where it was in his peripheral vision as he followed the speeder's taillights. When he thought he saw the stop sign it seemed further ahead and could have been the Roosevelt Boulevard stop sign illuminated by Wigglesworth's headlights. At that point the EDR data showed only a very slight acceleration of barely one-second duration, which was consistent with Higbee thinking there was still some distance for him to go before the actual intersection. Eventually, Ruth had to concede that within a second of when Higbee possibly could have seen the approaching van to his right, he slammed on his brakes.

That was crucial, since it totally refuted the testimony of the two Taylor witnesses who contended Higbee accelerated into the intersection. On my cross, Ruth had to admit: Rob's last few seconds of "hard braking" was "impact avoidance."

I had never seen nor spoken to Sgt. John McMahon before he was called to testify by Prosecutor Meyer. He had a military bearing, with crew cut and slate blue gray state police uniform. His demeanor revealed a very meticulous but confident individual. His answers were responsive, reflecting his almost 14 years with the state police, including eight with the Fatal Accident Unit.

He responded crisply without elaboration. His tone was more animated than Ulbrich but still appeared more like a math or science teacher than a police officer. He was well qualified to testify on accident reconstruction from many years of training and specialized education. I had no objection to his credentials, and the court easily accepted him as an expert. I had read McMahon's reports over and over for more than two years. I even had prepared poster board enlargements of some of his key paragraphs.

In accordance with court rules, the prosecutor and I exchanged all expert opinions and had pre-marked most of our exhibits in advance of trial to avoid surprises and delays. But just before his direct testimony was to begin, Prosecutor Meyer approached the court outside of the jury's hearing to object in advance to his own witness testifying to certain parts of his own report. Meyer claimed McMahon's conclusion "goes beyond his expertise." I believed he was referring to the exact paragraph I eventually intended to show the jury on the prepared exhibit.

The judge declared: "… well, I at least have a hunch as to what might be the objection by the prosecutor." I had written the judge a month before the trial and Meyer had known for years about my reliance on McMahon's observations of the faulty configuration of the intersection. The judge delayed ruling on the objection until after the direct examination. I knew the judge had some reservations about allowing any testimony about post remedial repairs and improvements to the intersection, which were noted in McMahon's report.

However, my whole defense case was premised on the explanation McMahon gave as to possible causation of the accident. He had observed the stop sign at Tuckahoe Road to be "further east than normal." All of my experts had agreed, and had given their opinions as to how Higbee could have made an honest mistake in his perception based upon the stop sign location at the time of the accident. McMahon made the first observation when he drove the route at night soon after the accident. I was shocked and disturbed that the judge might preclude me from asking the state's own expert about what McMahon had seen, when I had the chance to cross examine him.

On direct, the prosecutor attempted to bring out everything he thought would help his case, but carefully avoided McMahon's conclusions that did not support the theory of criminal "reckless behavior." The photographs and questions Meyer asked established the "visibility" of the stop sign—in daylight. McMahon was limited to describing the post of the stop sign as being on the east side of the curb lane of the approach with a widened shoulder.

McMahon was not allowed to describe how far to the right the sign was located, beyond the central vision of a driver. Meyer asked McMahon if the stop sign was visible from 350 feet before Tuckahoe Road, which it was, in daylight. Meyer tried to leave the jury with the impression that it was also clearly visible at night at a higher speed, which was not the case. Meyer also attempted to have McMahon support his theory that Higbee should have known where the stop sign was because he would have seen the backside of it as he turned south before he saw the speeder. That backfired, because when he showed McMahon the back of the sign in a photo, the careful investigator said he could not speculate that was the stop sign simply because it was silver in color and octagonal in shape without measuring it and studying the photograph.

Meyer's direct interrogation also brought out McMahon's calculations of speed based upon the impact measurements, the weight of the vehicles, and the road surface. McMahon calculated the speed of the girls' van was between 42 to 49 mph and Higbee's to be between 57 to 62 mph, both in a 35-mph zone. Meyer also brought out that Higbee's speed could have been as much as 64.89 miles per hour pre-impact per the EDR measurements. There was no electronic recording device in the Dodge van.

Next, Meyer tried to suggest some impropriety in Higbee's speeding to apprehend the violator. He asked McMahon to describe his knowledge of the "speed restriction" present in the law. I objected to the mis-characterization. The statute provides "exemptions to speed." The troopers and other police are permitted to exceed the speed limits when performing their duties as here. When the correction was made, McMahon was also asked about closing the gap without red lights and siren, and he responded Trooper Higbee "… was operating his vehicle properly." Finally when Meyer tried to have McMahon testify very narrowly about only the portions of his report that Meyer obviously thought might help his case, I offered to stipulate that McMahon's entire report could be submitted to the jury, without any objection by me. Meyer promptly refused, despite my argument in favor of "completeness." Now I was really worried about how much the judge might decide to limit my cross examination of Sgt. McMahon.

* * *

I had hoped to cross-examine Sgt. McMahon as soon as his lengthy direct concluded, but fate intervened. In the afternoon the jury had to be excused because of a family emergency for one of the jurors. So the judge and lawyers spent the rest of the day debating some of the legal arguments raised and deciding whether the prosecutor could call a witness, County Traffic Maintenance Supervisor Ron Hearon.

The next day, May 18, Sgt. McMahon's testimony resumed, but I was not able to conclude my cross examination so he was told to return Wednesday. That was trial day number nineteen and the fifth straight week of the proceedings. I wanted to go on, but the stress continued to build and I began to feel under the weather. I was so sick when I got to court that morning that even my adversary took pity on me and agreed to ask the judge for a day for me to recuperate. The judge refused to confer with us in chambers and had us argue in open court. I was frankly so sick I was afraid I would throw up on his bench as we stood before him in the courtroom. He gave me an hour to see if I was better. Investigator Ridgeway took me outside and emphatically convinced me I was doing a disservice to my client if I tried to push on. Reluctantly, and with Meyer's help convincing him, the judge adjourned the trial and I went home to sleep the rest of the day.

That night my brother Dave called me from California to say I looked like I was about to have a heart attack or a stroke from what he saw on the TV coverage for the day. When we returned the next day on Thursday, I returned the favor for Prosecutor Meyer's help. He wanted to have Richard Ruth testify out of order to save the cost of Ruth coming back to New Jersey a second time. I agreed and allowed Ruth's testimony before I finished my cross-examination of Sgt. John McMahon.

We all pushed to conclude Ruth's direct and cross-examination before the extended Memorial Day holiday. We all knew the jurors wanted to be off for the traditional start of the summer tourist season. Many jobs began that weekend when visitors made the trip "down the Shore" from nearby Philadelphia. Neither side wanted the jurors to be more upset with us.

The trial already was longer than expected, but because of the interruption, I got lucky. I resumed my cross of McMahon on the Tuesday after the holiday, but after Ruth had testified. I saw the chance to bring out holes in Ruth's one-sided presentation. By that time my energy had returned, but I had already lost some heated arguments with the court outside the presence of the jury. At one point, the judge declared: "What this case is not about is any contributory defect in the intersection."

When McMahon finally resumed the witness stand, the judge had ruled out any past history of accidents at the scene and any mention of "subsequent remedial measures" meaning improvements to the intersection. The judge further disallowed any testimony by McMahon that the stop sign was "further east than normal." In other words, I would not be able to have McMahon explain his theory of Higbee's mistake in perception. McMahon thought Trooper Higbee might be guilty of the traffic offense of careless driving because he missed the stop sign, but he found no reckless conduct, which was the state of mind required by vehicular homicide. I would not be permitted to put that in front of the jury in my questioning of McMahon.

I knew McMahon had retraced Higbee's approach and concluded it was reasonable that with the speed, darkness and difficult intersection Higbee had mistaken the Roosevelt Boulevard stop sign for the Tuckahoe Road sign. He had reported the closer sign to be six feet further to the right than would be expected. Moreover, utility poles concealed the small stop sign. Higbee had had less than a second to react to the potential of an impact at the crossing. None of that would come out to the jury, even though it was set forth in Sgt. McMahon's report to the prosecutor. I had to come up with another way to get these points across.

Just before the jury was to be called in, I asked Meyer's permission to briefly talk with McMahon before he came into the courtroom. With Meyer's okay, I entered the small witness waiting room to the side of the courtroom in which Sgt. McMahon was seated at a table, reading a book by Professor Olson. I was familiar with this book because I knew it was the text used by the Northwestern School of Accident Reconstruction. I had spoken by phone with Professor Olson long before the trial to seek advice. I knew McMahon had taken the Northwestern course because it was on his resume. We exchanged greetings, and I was able to alert him that I intended to go into only as much detail as I would be allowed, regarding the factors he took into account in his investigation.

Soon after he began to testify, I asked McMahon if he relied upon any textbooks and he produced the Olson book from his briefcase. As I continued my questioning, I leafed through the index and pulled out some definitions that I hoped would be helpful for the jury. For example, he was able to explain the theory of "driver expectation" taught in the course. If you see a "stop ahead sign" you will be looking for the stop sign up ahead. "Perception-reaction time" was a useful concept because McMahon could explain to the jury that you have to see something, understand what it is, and then be able to react appropriately. Even a well-trained trooper cannot improve on the minimum time it takes the human mind to perform that function. Rob's one-second reaction hitting the brakes was better than most.

Since the judge had prohibited me from using McMahon's word "normal," I tried two other words, suggested to me the night before by a longtime friend with many years in the legal system. I tried to have McMahon explain why the intersection was "unusual" or "confusing to motorists." I used the "Manual in Uniform Control Devices" to have McMahon confirm that the stop sign needed to be placed as close as possible to the roadway while "optimizing the visibility to the oncoming driver." The one at Tuckahoe Road was a full 22 feet from the center line, while the more visible one at Roosevelt Boulevard further ahead was only 16 feet to the right. I was not allowed to ask the witness about any changes to the intersection even though they were in his report. However, I was able to bring out that the stop sign at the time was the smallest in use, measuring at 30 inches, while an oversized sign is measured at 48 inches, designed to make it more visible. He was able to point out that there was only "ambient lighting" at the intersection at the time and that was a factor to be considered. I continued the questioning until the judge gave the jury a fifteen-minute mid-morning break.

With permission, I held on to the textbook by Olson. During that time, I quickly marked with little post-it notes some portions I would use for the rest of the questioning. McMahon told the jury about visibility and approaching vehicles. "Obscured vision" can occur with poles in front of a sign and oncoming vehicle headlights in the driver's eyes. McMahon also explained an object is more conspicuous if it is more brightly lit, against a dark contrast, is larger, and is directly in the sight line, rather than to the side of one's central vision. McMahon was allowed to supply a plausible explanation to the brief one-second of acceleration before Higbee hit the brakes. Higbee may have seen the Roosevelt Boulevard sign illuminated by Wigglesworth's headlights and thought there was more time and distance from the stop sign he was anticipating. He could not say this in so many words, but I hoped the jury could put it together from his theoretical explanation.

Likewise, I hoped the jury would conclude that as soon as Higbee might have realized something, the Dodge van, was coming to his right, just 2.2 seconds before the impact, Higbee slammed on the brakes. Naturally, McMahon was not allowed to say this, but I had laid the groundwork for that possible conclusion. By that time, the court adjourned for lunch. We hurried to our secret room on the second floor of the nearby Bellevue Restaurant, which was a half a block from the courthouse. It was the place we gathered away from any public or juror contact to talk.

When we returned to the courthouse, I again asked the judge to reconsider his earlier limiting rulings. He noticeably bit his lip, when I spoke of the impediment he had put on our proper defense. He castigated me with the critical comment that Sgt. McMahon, "just happened to have with him the textbook that you had already read and paginated off."

I resented the implication, but the judge insisted his "recollection was factually accurate" by which I guess he was suggesting some improper collusion with the witness. However, I was still not allowed to have the jury see or hear what Sgt. McMahon had put in his report about the stop sign at Stagecoach being "further right than normal." But, I was able to have the jury hear from him how the intersection appeared "unusual." McMahon was able to say the "wide-throated intersection" was "confusing," but that was as far as I could go. I could not ask McMahon his opinion on "causation" to advance my theory that this was simply a "mistake of fact" and not a deliberate wrongdoing.

I accused the judge of denying my client's right to a fair trial by refusing to permit a "causal analysis" by the qualified accident reconstructionist. I was able to let the jury know McMahon did not testify at the grand jury and he did not know Higbee was indicted until the day it was made public by Prosecutor Taylor. On redirect, Meyer tried to have McMahon testify Higbee should have been in a "state of readiness" approaching the intersection, suggesting some reckless behavior, but this time the judge ruled that was inappropriate. Meyer also tried to suggest Higbee would have seen the sign and stopped if he was traveling at "normal speed."

I tried to rebut that by showing Higbee was required to speed to do his duty. Further, his "reaction time," as well as his perception, was affected by his focus on the taillights of Wigglesworth's car. The day ended with some of what I wanted to bring out, but with a lot of unconnected dots for the jury to figure out at the end of the case. I had promised the jury in my opening they would hear about the defective intersection, but I was not sure they really heard enough to picture it.

Chapter 10

Day 22, week number six of the trial. The prosecution was finally winding down. Rob and I and our trial team were alert to the probability that Meyer wanted to end his case on an emotional note, to evoke sympathy for the victims. The next witness was to be the acting medical examiner for the region. The female pathologist who performed the original autopsies had left the area and the prosecutor wanted to introduce her report by having this new expert review the findings even though he never viewed the bodies himself. Ordinarily, I could object and try to force the state to produce the original doctor. I sought to limit the testimony anyway, and knew his opinion would have to stay within the confines of the original autopsy reports, so I did not object when Dr. Charles F. Siebert, Jr., M.D. was qualified to give his opinion as to the causes of the deaths.

Dr. Siebert appeared to be in his fifties, heavy-set, receding hairline, with a slightly graying mustache and goatee. His manner was quite professional, consistent with his qualifications. The judge instructed the jury that the doctor's opinion in the field of Forensic Pathology could be considered according to the jury's own determination, as with any expert. We knew the prosecutor wanted to introduce photos of the girls taken at the scene. Understandably that would evoke terrible feelings for the victim's mother. We hoped that Meyer could prevail upon her to leave the courtroom for this next testimony, even though she had an absolute right to be there if she so chose. An emotional outburst needed to be avoided if possible.

Fortunately, Maria Caiafa was not present when Dr. Siebert testified. He described in rather grotesque detail the multiple injuries sustained by the victims, but in a methodical and unemotional presentation. The causes of death were "multiple blunt force traumas" for both victims. Prosecutor Meyer then wanted to introduce several frightful photographs of the victims taken at the scene showing the effects of the injuries. In my opinion, these photographs had the capacity to be so prejudicial as to overcome any real probative value in the case. So, at side bar, I argued with the prosecutor and judge against admitting them to be seen by the jury. The photos added nothing to the testimony of the expert. Even if I lost this argument, I needed the record to reflect my objection, so that if Rob were convicted, an appellate court might consider the judge's ruling to be reversible error. I lost the argument.

The judge permitted these horrific photographs to be circulated, that is, passed from one juror to the other while seated in the jury box, so each would be able to look at them up close. We watched carefully, as the exhibits were passed along from one juror to the next. Most took a very quick look, some with concern and perhaps even irritation. No one gave more than a passing glance at either photograph. That suggested to me that perhaps they also regarded the photos to be redundant and not necessary in view of the doctor's testimony. The jurors obviously tried to adhere to the judge's instruction to not show any outward emotion or reaction.

Dr. Seibert's medical opinion was the deaths were due to an accident due to the totality of the circumstances. He defined accident as "an unforeseen event that causes a person's death." The prosecutor wanted the jury to be told this medical opinion had "no legal significance," but the judge declined. On cross-examination, the doctor conceded that the multiple injuries sustained by both driver and passenger were due not only to the various impacts with the automobiles, but also to the collision between the two sisters.

Examination of the injuries corroborated the conclusion that the heavier passenger was not wearing her seatbelt. No one could determine the precise timing of the injuries to any medical degree of probability. Therefore, the cause of death was due to not only the impact of the collision of the automobiles, but also the impact of one victim upon the other. It was said, but could not be emphasized, for fear the jury might think the defense was blaming the victims for the tragic accident. The expert was excused, and the state rested its case.

It was the middle of the day, and we had stayed up the night before, preparing a legal argument for the judge, anticipating this moment. The jury was led out of the courtroom. We had to preserve our rights in case of appeal and to tell the judge why there should be a dismissal at this point. But everyone knew the law required the judge to give the prosecution the benefit of "all favorable inferences." We had little hope the judge would take the case away from the jury to decide.

As expected, the prosecutor argued he had supplied all elements of the crime in evidence. Despite no expert opinions, he said Higbee did not operate his vehicle as a "reasonable law enforcement officer" should have done under all of the circumstances. He argued that Rob "knew or should have known" of the stop sign's exact location and he "grossly" exceeded the speed limit, trying to apprehend the speeder. The judge seemed to adopt the same argument Meyer had made to Barry Wythe and me before the indictment. Higbee should have realized where the stop sign was because he had just passed the backside of the sign going in the opposite direction a few minutes before. Higbee could, therefore, be considered "reckless" and guilty of vehicular homicide. Judge Batten denied our motion for acquittal and we had to begin our defense case that afternoon.

One of the arguments Meyer had presented during his case was to suggest that Rob was merely "dazed" during the accident. He could claim Rob was "aware of his surroundings." That way, Meyer could say in summation Higbee, "consciously disregarded a known risk" and deliberately lied when he said he thought he had stopped at the intersection. In order to show Rob's state of mind, we needed evidence of his condition.

Both sides knew Higbee was diagnosed with a concussion after the accident. I persuaded Meyer to allow a stipulation as to his diagnosis, instead of incurring the expense of calling medical witnesses. We provided the judge with our written agreement as to Rob's injuries. The court instructed the jury as to the continuing presumption of innocence; the defendant has no burden to prove anything, and he need not testify. We called our first witness, knowing the jury would expect us to disprove any factor the prosecutor claimed to be evidence of guilt.

The prosecutor had not called Janet Harmelin, the nurse who was passing by after the accident. We wanted to show Rob's condition immediately after the accident to explain his faulty memory of the events that had just taken place. In describing the scene, she almost broke down and cried, but paused and recovered her composure. She described Trooper Higbee as only "semi-conscious" and "not alert." He was constantly trying to reach for his radio, as he lay in the driver's seat when she first saw him. She stayed with him until the arrival of the first emergency responders.

Chief Jay Newman was my next witness that same afternoon. He appeared in his official crisp white shirt with badge and blue uniform of the Marmora Fire Department. Investigator Manny Ridgeway and I had briefed him repeatedly about the judge's rulings concerning the intersection. We warned him again before he came into court not to talk of previous accidents or any of the remedial changes Newman sought from the county.

On September 27, 2006 Chief Newman answered his pager and radioed his response to the Ocean City Dispatcher shortly after 10:00 p.m. The call was to "Route 9 and Tuckahoe Road." I asked him: "What did you do in response to that dispatch, sir?" "I left my house," he told the jury. En route he called his deputy chief to respond to the second place where Tuckahoe Road intersects Route 9 a few miles north at Beesley's Point, just in case that was the correct location. He saw no sign of an accident when he arrived at Route 9 and Tuckahoe Road, which was minutes from his home. Finding nothing where he was first sent, he turned left on Tuckahoe and volunteered in his answer: "I went to Stagecoach and Tuckahoe Road where several incidents had occurred before, so I figured that is where this would end up."

There was neither objection by the prosecutor nor any action by the judge. When I asked him to please describe "the illumination" at the intersection when he found the accident, Newman stated it was "a poorly lit intersection," with only one streetlight pointing away from the northbound stop sign at Stagecoach. "I am familiar with the intersection," he continued. "When you approach from the south, the Roosevelt stop sign is more visible and you cannot see the one at Tuckahoe until just before you are on it." Again, the prosecutor made no objection, nor did the judge comment.

I was about to introduce photographs to attempt to illustrate his testimony for the jury. The prosecutor asked for both of us to approach the judge's bench and the judge motioned us up. The discussion took place out of the hearing of the jury, but the court had provided Rob with headphones at the counsel table so he could listen to each of these conversations as he had a right to hear everything. No one else could hear us except for the court reporter close by. Meyer objected to Newman telling the jury of "prior accidents." I corrected him and said Newman mentioned only "several incidents."

Meyer claimed he did not voice his objection at the time as a matter of strategy since he did not want to call the jury's attention to prior accidents when approaching the intersection. The judge adamantly criticized me personally for allowing Newman to give an opinion, which he said happened three times, referring to "one street light" and "poorly lit." He also criticized the testimony, which had indicated that the stop sign at Tuckahoe Road was further to the right than it normally would be. He fumed that these were previously declared off limits and this was a deliberate attempt to get around his rulings.

The judge commented that the opinion was not warranted by Newman's expertise and he was only being called as a fact witness, not a qualified expert. Further, the use of the word "normal" was not warranted under the situation and the jury would not be able to understand the word. The prosecutor then did what no one had tried to do to me in over forty years of trial work. "I move to hold Mr. Subin in contempt of court."

The judge responded he would readily consider the application, but would postpone any hearing on the request until the end of the trial rather than delay the proceedings. The judge has the power to control all court proceedings in his presence, including disciplining attorneys who violate any rules. But a summary contempt of court would still require a hearing before the judge to determine if my conduct was so egregious and outside the bounds of ethical propriety as to warrant imposing sanctions. The judge could impose monetary fines on me, or he could immediately incarcerate me. He could order the sheriff to put me in handcuffs and whisk me away to the county jail. I pleaded with him I had taken every precaution to avoid testimony in violation of his previous rulings. I suspected the prosecutor was using this as a tactic to try to intimidate me, but I still had to vigorously defend my client and urge the admissibility of evidence that was crucial to our defense.

At that moment I thought back to the unwarranted opinion evidence brought out by various prosecution witnesses. Robert Taylor said Trooper Higbee was, "driving crazy." His son Michael accused Higbee of "putting pedal to the metal." I was infuriated by this latest dilemma. I wanted to quote from Jack Nicholson's character in the movie, *A Few Good Men* and exclaim: "You can't handle the truth!" But I bit my tongue and kept that thought to myself. Rob was listening through the headphones at counsel table and relayed his concerns to the rest of our trial team.

At a break, when my wife learned of the threat of jail, she tried to joke about it. Maybe a good night's sleep in the holding cell might do me some good, she quipped. But I reminded her that small, old attorneys don't do well inside a jail. I tried to laugh it off, but inside I was deeply concerned.

We concluded Newman's testimony very carefully and limited what he could tell the jury. The next morning I woke up about 3:00 a.m. That had occurred almost every day for about two years since Higbee had been indicted. It was a recurring nightmare: *This fine man would go to prison because I had failed.* This time the dream was worse. I was in a sweat and paced the bedroom floor trying not to wake my wife. What if I was thrown in jail and could not continue to represent Rob? Who would take over? The threat of *contempt of court* was to hang over me for the rest of the trial.

Chapter 11

Geoffrey Loftus was called by the defense on May 28, 2009. White haired, mannerly, and kindly looking, he looks like what you would expect of the learned college professor. He is the chairman of the Department of Psychology at the University of Washington in Seattle, and has taught there for 37 years. His education includes studies at Brown, Stanford, and New York Universities. He is internationally recognized for his publications and presentations on perception, memory, and related fields. The court accepted him as an expert. Professor Loftus spoke to the jury as if they were students in a seminar. He added to his presentation with colorful power point and graphs to illustrate his conclusions. His answers were crisp and clear, and he patiently explained the terms he used.

Perception of an event may consist of "fragments of information" that we see and hear. Over time some fragments are lost, and that is *"forgetting."* Memory also changes because of *"post event information."* Your perceptions of an event may later be influenced by media accounts of that event or by hearing others describe it. Much of what we remember is also influenced by how we observed the original event. How close was the witness? Was it dark or light? How quickly did it happen? How well does the person see or hear? The further away from the incident in time and space, the less likely the memory is really correct. Reorganization occurs. We all like complete explanations. We tend to "connect the dots" in our minds for completeness.

When you look at an Impressionist painting, you make sense out of lights and shadows, and often what you see on the canvas is not really there. When a witness is trying to describe an event from memory it may seem to be "real-seeming" and the witness may seem very confident in his or her conclusions. But over time, those recollections may have become more inaccurate. The witness really believes that is what was seen or heard. But post event influences may make someone believe they saw or heard something that they did not. Professor Loftus pointed out that if you are paying attention, you are probably trying to accomplish some goal. You are focused on that task. You may be bombarded with outside information from the surrounding environment. If you are not paying attention to those bits of information you probably will not remember them later. If there is no need to notice insignificant details you will not remember them. Perhaps that is why the Taylors in their Mazda did not take notice of the Wigglesworth vehicle passing them in the opposite direction before the accident.

When outside influences are competing, your attention is divided. You may not process a crucial bit of information like a specific sight or sound. Professor Loftus told the jury of an experiment he conducted on post-incident influences. A film was shown to two groups. It showed a two-car collision. The first test group was asked to estimate how fast the vehicles were going when they "hit" each other. The second was asked to make the estimate of speed when the cars "smashed" into each other. The second group had higher estimates of speed. In the second phase of the experiment Loftus explained the two groups were asked: "Did you see any broken glass in the film?" The group who were given the suggestive word "smashed" was more likely to have reported seeing broken glass when there was none in the film.

Inferential memory factors may have contributed to Michael Taylor's conclusion that Higbee was accelerating into the intersection, when the circumstantial data refuted that conclusion. Stressful events can result in even more difficulty capturing the accurate details in memory. In explaining how we seem to add in facts that are really not there, Loftus told of another experiment. The test subjects were shown pictures of a woman shopping in a supermarket. She was faced with a carefully organized pile of oranges and appeared to be reaching her hand out as if to pick one from the pile. Another in the series of photos depicted her standing in front of the oranges strewn on the entire floor in front of her. Later the group was asked if they had seen a picture of the woman picking the orange from the pile. Most of the group said yes. They had wrongly concluded they must have seen her pull an orange from the middle of the pile. They were confident in their memories, though their recollections were inaccurate. They were not lying; they honestly believed that they were accurately recalling what they saw in the photo.

Professor Loftus told with graphic illustrations that you only see in a narrow field of vision called "central vision," when you are focused on an object straight in front of you. Objects to the side in "peripheral vision" do not enable you to take appropriate actions as easily and quickly as those immediately in your focus. Apply that theory to the last six seconds before the accident, and it becomes obvious that Trooper Higbee saw the Roosevelt Boulevard sign more clearly in his central vision than the one at the fatal intersection. If you add the darkness of night to the equation, Loftus concluded Higbee would not have seen the stop sign off to his peripheral vision because it was not "moving, big, or bright."

Central vision is only about two degrees of the 360 degrees attainable if you were to move your head all the way around. The 30" stop sign at Tuckahoe Road was not in Higbee's central vision. The 36" stop sign at Roosevelt Boulevard was lit by the reflection of Josh Wigglesworth's headlights, and would appear closer to Higbee than it really was. That accounted for the brief period of acceleration before Higbee slammed on his brakes. Higbee was focused on the taillights moving away from him in his central vision. It would have been very difficult to pick out the small stop sign far to his right in peripheral vision. When he did slam on his brakes, it may have been that he spotted the Becker girls' van, because it was "big, bright and moving" even though in his peripheral vision.

Loftus pointed out that average reaction time is 1.5 seconds for a driver to see an object, make a decision, and take appropriate action. Higbee applied the brakes within 1 second, but he could not avoid the impact. When asked about Higbee's post accident statement, Loftus explained it was probably "faulty memory," which was the product of the influences described previously. Upon cross-examination, Meyer tried to inject the term "falsified memory" into his question, but my objection was sustained. Professor Loftus had supplied an alternative to the prosecutor's theory of a deliberate disregard of a known approaching hazard.

One last example used by Loftus served to explain "tunnel vision" as a reason this was an accident not a crime. Professor Loftus had the jury picture a center fielder focusing on catching a high fly ball amidst the lights of a night baseball game. As he kept his eye on the ball while running with outstretched glove he runs into the fence. Did he do so deliberately or did he make a mistake in perception? I hoped the explanation by Professor Loftus was the beginning of the downfall of the prosecutor's attempt to convict Trooper Higbee based upon the theory the trooper consciously disregarded the risk of causing serious bodily injury or death.

Lt. Col. Frank Rodgers, New Jersey State Police (Ret.) had served as acting superintendent and held almost every other rank since he began his career many years earlier as a road trooper. He had been in charge of various sensitive areas such as organized crime and corruption and handled numerous internal affairs investigations. He had no hesitation in pursuing criminal or disciplinary charges against any trooper who deliberately engaged in wrongdoing. His track record of enforcing the strict standards of accountability in the state police was impeccable. When I asked Frank Rodgers to step forward to the witness stand the next morning I knew that the prosecutor had no one to rebut Rodgers' expertise. That was important, because a key issue in the case was whether Rob Higbee acted as "a reasonable law enforcement officer" in the circumstances.

Thanks to the early ruling of Judge Alvarez that was the standard by which Higbee's conduct would be measured, I could now use that to my advantage to provide an opinion that Trooper Higbee did not deviate from that standard. Frank Rodgers has the bearing of a military general. He has closely cropped grayish-white hair, but still appears athletic and trim in his build. He was neatly dressed with white shirt, gold tie, and dark suit. Despite his erect bearing, he spoke calmly and carefully, almost soft-spoken, but extremely articulate. He focused his attention directly on the jury while listening intently to every question posed to him. He explained his method-ical review of every state police standard operating procedure, rule, or regulation that might have applied to Higbee's actions. He told the jury that Higbee was "closing the gap" and not engaging in a "pursuit."

Rodgers also made it abundantly clear that the protocols were orders to the more than four-thousand state police. These were not permissive guidelines. A trooper follows orders when he refrains from using red lights and sirens until he can safely identify and pull over the vehicle. If the individual then ignores his instructions or signals, and chooses to flee, it becomes a pursuit. There were only 415 pursuits which had to be approved by a supervisor, as opposed to three-quarter of a million closing the gap situations in New Jersey in the three years before the accident. Pursuits are only authorized after the suspect has demonstrated a clear intent to elude or resist apprehension. Lt. Col. Rodgers said unequivocally, "Trooper Higbee was doing exactly as he had been trained to do, exactly as he was expected to do" when he attempted to close the gap on the speeder without red lights and siren. He also pointed out there was no real incentive to apprehend a speeder. It is part of his duties, but troop-ers are encouraged to issue warnings and avoid summonses when-ever possible.

Furthermore, Rodgers testified that protocol demanded a trooper to maintain continuous eye contact with a suspected viola-tor, to provide proper proof of identification of the driver and vehi-cle. When Higbee made his K-turn he had to focus on the rapidly disappearing taillights of the car he'd previously clocked on radar. Higbee's tracking of the target vehicle is "what I would have done," declared Rodgers. When cross-examined by the prosecutor about the obligation to public safety, Rodgers said that in this instance public safety is synonymous with the safety of the officer. He ac-knowledged troopers are not exempt from obeying stop signs, but troopers are human beings, and this intersection was not well marked. Rodgers stated: "I find absolutely no deviation from any policy and procedures. The only thing I find is that it was a terrible accident. Some of the contributing factors were beyond Trooper Higbee's control."

Meyer repeatedly tried to shake the testimony, contending Higbee was "doing twice the speed limit" attempting to pursue the vehicle. Lt. Col. Rodgers calmly replied that Higbee's speed was only five miles over the speeder's 65 miles per hour caught on radar, as Higbee was attempting to close the gap. Higbee's Ford Crown Victoria Police package was capable of 120 miles per hour. Higbee's speed was reasonable I could later argue. When the prosecutor attacked Higbee's credibility from the statement he gave to the investigators, Rodgers countered that Sgt. Ulbrich had concluded Higbee was not being deceptive when he gave the statement. Higbee always qualified his account with expressions like, "to the best of my recollection." He had no independent recall of the exact moments of the crash.

Like all NJSP members, Higbee knew the specialized Fatal Accident Unit carefully investigated every fatal accident. He noted that in the same Troop A area about two or three weeks before Higbee's accident EDR data was obtained from a GM patrol car involved in an accident. Clearly, Higbee knew every pre-collision movement would be meticulously analyzed by any means possible. Higbee did not lie; he believed he would have stopped and looked both ways at a stop sign.

Meyer asked: "Shouldn't a reasonable trooper substantially reduce the speed prior to the intersection after he had seen a warning of the upcoming stop sign?" Rodgers replied that he had traced the pre-impact approach based upon Sgt. McMahon's analysis. Rodgers concluded that the Roosevelt stop sign was more within the "central vision" of Trooper Higbee who might well have mistaken that stop sign for the one at Tuckahoe Road, implying that was the reason his speed was not substantially reduced at that precise moment. Meyer tried to suggest Higbee's speed alone amounted to "reckless" conduct. Rodgers pointed out the speed was justified under the speed law exemption for police.

"There's no way to catch up with a speeder we are trying to apprehend" unless the trooper exceeds the violator's speed. That surely seemed logical to me. Rodgers pointed out that Higbee was only semi-familiar with the intersection and might not have seen the stop sign in his peripheral vision. "No rational police officer is going to go through a stop sign based upon my training and experience." He did everything a "reasonable law enforcement officer" would do.

Rodgers concluded Higbee may have seen the van in his peripheral vision to his right and immediately slammed on his brakes. Not only was there no "gross deviation" as the prosecutor asserted, but Rodgers concluded there was no deviation from any policies or procedures of the state police. Rodgers concluded Higbee was the victim of a series of unfortunate contributing factors that led to the fatalities. These included the dynamics of the intersection, the speed of the vehicles, and the lack of seatbelt by the passenger in the van. Given the circumstances, Trooper Higbee could not ignore his duty. The speeder might turn out to be a wanted felon. The trooper had to try to find out why he was going almost twice the limit on this dark road. The accident was an "honest mistake" and might well have happened to Rodgers.

Watching the jurors during the testimony, I believe Rodgers' unchallenged integrity and experienced authority resonated among them. There would be no rebuttal expert for the prosecution to establish that Higbee's actions were a gross deviation from that which a reasonable law enforcement officer would do. The prosecutor still had the burden of proof to show that Higbee was reckless to establish vehicular homicide. I could argue, at the end of the case, that we had just disproved that element.

Chapter 12

Trooper Rob Higbee had just turned 37 the day he faced his accusers in his own defense. Even though we did not inform the judge or the media until it was revealed in open court, we actually decided in advance of the trial that he would testify. Not only would he be a persuasive witness, but the prosecutor could legally introduce his prior statement to the investigators anyway, and we wanted Rob to explain any inconsistencies based upon his faulty memory of the accident. We did not fear cross-examination because the trooper had an unblemished record in the New Jersey State Police.

His testimony was to be a combination of courage, professionalism and compassion. Maria Caiafa, the girls' mother, moved up to the front row instead of the seat she usually had sat in for the entire trial. She was seated directly in the sight of the witness from behind the prosecutor's table. Every time Rob was to look toward the prosecutor he would see her, and so would the jury. I needed Rob to demonstrate his strength of character and yet admit to human frailties that may have led to a terrible mistake in judgment. It was after all, Higbee's state of mind that would show he was innocent of criminal wrongdoing.

I spent some time in questioning Rob to bring out his past accomplishments in his life, despite his reluctance. His undergraduate degree in history from the University of Delaware, ability to teach, outstanding records in basketball and football competition were all to show the decent individual he was. I also knew that the prosecutor would attack his credibility and I was setting the stage for character witnesses who would speak to his honesty and integrity the

next day. I also focused on the extensive training he received from
the state police. I had Rob personally explain his understanding of
"closing the gap" as opposed to "pursuit" and how he tried to adhere to all of the state police orders and protocols that night.

He explained what had happened, just as he had in his statement
in October of 2006. Again, he could not recall the exact instants before the impact. He conceded he did not know whether he actually
stopped for the stop sign. He admitted, upon review of the circumstantial evidence, that he apparently had not, but Rob turned to the
jury, and in a firm and convincing manner said: *"In no way would I
ever intentionally disregard a stop sign."*

I paused to be sure the jury got the impact of that statement. I
had to anticipate the prosecutor's cross-examination to follow. Why
did Higbee say to the investigators that he thought he had stopped
and looked both ways before the crash? "There is no way I would
deliberately lie," Higbee told the jury. His recollection of the event
was no different today than then.

But he admitted that his memory could well be faulty. He put
together the pieces of his recollection of that night as best he could
to help the investigation. Higbee emphatically told the jury: *"Never.
Never would I consciously disregard or go through a stop sign. I have
never done it ever—ever in my life, let alone on patrol while working."*

I asked him if there was any policy or procedure of the NJSP
that would justify deliberately going through a stop sign. He responded had he perceived the stop sign, he would have slowed
down, and put on his emergency red lights and proceeded through
the intersection after checking both ways. This was a critical moment to convey to the jury. Higbee would never decide to go
through a stop sign.

The judge, with only a slight apology, interrupted my direct examination of Higbee. He saw his secretary in the back of the courtroom and had her come up to the bench to receive a note from him.
She departed. But the dramatic flow of the testimony had been interrupted for some unknown reason. The impact of the testimony
having been somewhat diluted, I turned to other issues. Did Higbee
attempt to close the gap in his memory of the accident? What I really asked him was to tell the jury what he did to recreate the scene

in his mind so he might better remember what he saw that night.

Higbee began to describe what he observed when we returned to the scene with our various experts. Just then the prosecutor rose to object. Meyer and I went to sidebar to speak with the judge. Meyer claimed I was attempting to have my client give "expert testimony" about the intersection, for which he was unqualified. I said my client should be allowed to testify as to what he saw, especially because of Sgt. McMahon's observations in his report.

It looked like a long argument, so the judge sent the jury to a separate room so we could argue in open court. Prosecutor Meyer objected to any evidence by Higbee that would suggest an "alternative explanation." He reminded the judge that Higbee had just testified on direct that he remembered "approaching, braking, looking, and darkness."

We wanted Higbee to describe the confusing nature of the approach that he saw upon returning to the scene. The judge had already told us we could not refer to the stop sign as further to the side than "normal." But McMahon testified to the "unusual, wide throated intersection" and Loftus to the sight line to Roosevelt Boulevard. Why could not Higbee indicate he saw it as well?

At one point the discussion resulted in my expressing my concern that, "The truth has been suppressed by the court in the observation of one approaching the intersection." If the judge did not allow this testimony, I said Higbee was being denied a fair trial.

The judge relented a little and said he would allow Higbee to describe what the Roosevelt Boulevard sign looked like when he saw it again. Meyer tried to preclude that, stating perhaps that sign had been changed as well, and we could not talk about any improvements. I challenged him since we could prove the 36" stop sign at Roosevelt Boulevard closer to the center line has a date of installation on it of 2004 as observed by my Investigator Ridgeway. Meyer backed down.

Higbee was allowed to tell the jury, that when he had returned to review the scene at night, the larger stop sign at Roosevelt Boulevard was in his central vision. That stop sign was in a direct sight line versus the one at Tuckahoe Road, which was off to the right of his view. We were allowed to refer to some of the same photographs

Professor Loftus used. I then asked Higbee why he returned to the scene. When Rob answered this question I caught a trace of emotion in his otherwise stoic and even presentation. He looked right at the girls' mother when he said, "I thought about it thousands of times and I wanted to know why it may have occurred, why it happened. And I need those answers, just as some people may need those answers."

At this point I wanted Rob to tell what was going through his mind at that same place the night of the accident. After more objections, but with permission of the judge, Rob explained that in September 2006 he had just gotten married and was planning a family. He and his wife Beth had "everything to live for." His objective that fateful night was: "…to do my job to the best of my ability, and I tried to do that, given all the circumstances. But as I know since then, something occurred, a mistake and a terrible accident occurred. There would be no reason for me to enter an intersection without knowing what was coming the other way, without caution." He went on to say, "I know a terrible accident occurred and I can't bring back what happened with that accident."

Meyer's cross-examination of Higbee was laborious, tedious, misleading and largely ineffective. He kept trying to suggest that Higbee should have known the exact location of the stop sign because he should have noticed the backside of it when he turned down the street. Meyer implied that a "reasonable" officer would slow down, to which Rob responded, "Only if the officer recognized a stop sign was present."

Meyer wanted to suggest that Higbee was only chasing a young speeding driver. Higbee responded that he could not know what offense might have been committed. He could be coming from a robbery, an assault, or some other crime. "We are taught that we don't know who the person is and to approach all persons who are potential violators of the law, with due caution."

Meyer also tried to say Rob should have been able to perceive all objects around him, including the stop sign and the approaching van because of his training and his enhanced peripheral vision from sports. "Apples and oranges" was the abbreviated response. The essence of Rob Higbee's testimony was he had thought about the incident more than "a thousand times" and could only conclude it was a terrible accident. He would never consciously disregard danger to life by ignoring a stop sign.

Everyone in the courtroom was riveted on Rob Higbee and on Maria Caiafa, when he gazed directly into her eyes and talked about the crash: *"It's the first thing I think about when I get up in the morning. It's the last thing I think about when I go to bed at night. I think about it when I'm alone. I think about it when I'm with my daughter. I don't know if I'll ever get past this, because long after this proceeding, I'll still be living with this event."*

* * *

The concept of character witnesses in a criminal trial is a bit of an anomaly. On the defense, we are not allowed to put a defendant's good character in evidence unless he has already testified and the prosecution has put on some challenge to his credibility. Here, the prosecutor tried to suggest that Higbee lied in his October 2006 statement when he said he thought he'd stopped and looked both ways. Now that Rob Higbee had testified, I wanted the jury to hear what a truthful, honest individual he was thought to be in his community. That opinion evidence of his reputation is all we are permitted to tell the jury. No witness can come forward with any specific instances of good conduct observed. Since we were in the seventh week of trial, I had no intention of delaying the case, so I tried to fit in all of the witnesses we had lined up in Rob's behalf for the morning of June 2, 2009.

Thanks to Investigator Manny Ridgeway, all of the witnesses were briefed, lined up in order of appearance outside of the courtroom, and brought in one by one in rapid succession to accommodate the time constraints. We had over 100 persons who had told us they wanted to testify in Rob's behalf, but we finally narrowed the number to thirty-nine so we could fit them in. Every one of them was required to simply identify himself or herself, how they knew Rob, for how long, and then give an opinion of Rob's reputation in the community. That opinion had to be limited to traits relating to truthfulness, honesty and integrity and like descriptions.

That was the only testimony permitted, according to our Rules of Court. Some examples of the spectrum of the community we produced were: Regional Superintendent of Schools Dr. Dan Loggi, Linwood Mayor Richard DiPamphillis; and various friends and neighbors, all of whom said Rob's integrity was beyond reproach. George Evinski, the longtime Mainland High School director of athletics exclaimed that in his fifty years of teaching: "Rob was one of the most outstanding young men that I have ever met in my life." Bob Coffey, with twenty-four years as head football coach at Mainland High School, referred to Rob as "a gentle giant" and "one of my favorites of all time."

A former employer, local restaurant owner Dennis D'Orio, Dr. Gerald Abbott, business owners, sales representatives, and "stay-at-home-moms" spoke about Rob's honesty. Jack Boyd and his wife Rita, both teachers at Ocean City High School knew Rob well. Mr. Boyd coached high school basketball teams Rob had competed against all through high school. He declared Rob is, "a person I would love to have as a son." Another competitor, Tyrone Rolls, now an Ocean City police officer, had played football for Ocean City against Rob and had told me Rob was the kind of guy who would block you hard, but then turn around and help you up to be sure you were okay. He was not allowed to say that in court, but he spoke of Rob's credibility. We tried to include old, young, male, female, residents of Cape May and Atlantic Counties, and various racial, ethnic, and religious backgrounds to show the jury that admiration for Rob's integrity was not confined to a small or narrow group in the area.

Everyone who knew him described how forthright Rob is at all times. He would never lie. Michael Tangradi, a union carpenter testified, "Rob is the most honest person I have ever met—bar none." Present and former state troopers from New Jersey and Pennsylvania who knew Rob talked about him as being "honest in everything he did." Complete candor is a rigid requirement in the rules of the NJSP, and eleven-year-veteran Detective Jim Hoopes spoke of Rob as having the "utmost character and integrity" of any person he has ever met. Rob's "impeccable reputation" was brought out by his wife's employer John Heist, whose insurance business is known throughout Cape May County. Joe Rich, Jr., a retired plumbing and fire prevention company president, wanted to be prepared to answer the question of Rob's standing in the community, so he talked with people for four months before the trial everywhere in the area and stated: "Not one person whom I've talked to has anything bad to say about Rob," despite the huge media attack on Rob for the past few years. Ken Williams, retired educator and three-sport coach at Mainland testified: "In my twenty-eight years of teaching, he may be one of the finest students I've ever had. Very honest and trustworthy. I'd be proud to have Rob as my son." I asked if others in the area shared this opinion. He responded: "Well, it's obvious from the people here today that shows." I watched for reactions from the jurors, but they all tried hard to maintain poker faces. I did turn around to the audience and caught a glimpse of my own wife who had tears in her eyes and a smile of admiration for this testimonial for Rob.

Most of the time Meyer simply waived cross-examination of the witness. He did so this time also, but quickly adjusted his glasses and peered down at his papers, showing no reaction to the jury. Some witnesses spoke of telling their children to emulate Rob and look up to him for his responsibility and integrity. Throughout these proceedings Rob tried hard to maintain an expressionless face. But his slight smile of appreciation was obvious to most as they passed our counsel table on their way out of the courtroom. Rob felt awkward and uncomfortable having all of these people come to court on his behalf, but I assured him how insistent they were to be there for him.

One of the last witnesses I called that morning was one of the most persuasive in my opinion. Daniel Williams is the nephew of Coach Kenny Williams, and the son of retired Judge Richard Williams, who was Administrative Director of the Courts for New Jersey. But it was Dan's poise and confident bearing that I believe most impressed the jury. Dan went to Dickinson College and Widener Law School, but gave up the practice of law for his passion —teaching. He grew up with Rob and was the other 1,000-point career scorer on the basketball team. Dan Williams not only said Rob was "extremely truthful" and has "tons of integrity," but he added:

"He is the most truthful person and of the utmost character of any person I have ever met." The number of persons in the courtroom and who testified indicated the support he had in the community. I thought this summed up what I wanted the jury to hear. I wanted the character witnesses to bolster the thought that Rob Higbee did not and never would lie, to eliminate the prosecutor's attack on Rob's credibility. We needed to remove the last impediment to a belief that Rob was innocent.

I saved my final witness for the afternoon of June 2, 2009. Bruce Siddle was known internationally for his studies and writings on "critical incident amnesia" which explained the faulty memory of those in stressful situations. I deliberately put Siddle on after Higbee and his character witnesses had made clear he would not lie. But why would a trained police officer not remember correctly what happened in the moments before the impact? If he didn't lie to the investigators, why would he think he really stopped and looked both ways when we know now he did not? What factors impinged upon his memory?

Professor Loftus gave the jury a scientific explanation. Lt. Col. Rodgers said Higbee followed NJSP procedures, but I still wanted the jury to understand that even the best trained individual may make honest mistakes in perception and judgment without criminal intent. I also wanted them to know even the most skilled and well-trained police and military officers may not remember details in a critical and stressful incident.

I located Bruce Siddle in Illinois based upon a recommendation from a respected New Jersey law enforcement official who had seen his training program. Siddle was a former police officer, and had provided advice to such diverse groups as the CIA, U.S. Navy Seals, Queen's Guards in England, Hong Kong Police, and special forces throughout the world. He has particularly focused on shooting incidents, but also was familiar with split second reactions in auto crashes. As he approached the stand, I thought back to when I first had contacted him. He was appropriately skeptical, and would not agree to provide an expert opinion until he had thoroughly reviewed all reports and statements and completely debriefed my client. In addition, he also flew to New Jersey and carefully retraced the approach to the intersection at night. He had to be absolutely convinced of the authenticity of our position before he made a judgment.

Even the night before when we had gone over his anticipated testimony, Siddle seemed strangely nervous. When I inquired, he told me this case had taken on more of a meaning to him than many others. He had become personally convinced of Trooper Higbee's innocence. He did not want to miss anything in his analysis. He did not want to do anything that would jeopardize a jury finding of "Not Guilty." Siddle told me he felt the significance of this case for law enforcement throughout the country. Many officers he had investigated were second-guessed about fatalities resulting from proper discharge of their weapons. Accidental shootings of innocent persons have resulted even when an officer is totally justified using deadly force to prevent death or serious bodily harm. Immediately after those incidents, some officers could not honestly recall how many shots were fired or remember hearing outside noises during the incident.

Siddle's research reminded me of another expert I had consulted, a retired Philadelphia police detective who also devoted his post police employment to investigation of similar incidents. The detective told me when he was on the job in Philadelphia he was in a high-speed pursuit of a wanted fugitive when the car ahead crashed very near to his patrol car snapping a telephone pole. He had absolutely no recollection of hearing any noise. His concentration on the car ahead did not permit access to the loud crashing sound in his memory. He had a "faulty recollection" of that incident. We needed to explain this phenomenon.

With all this in mind, I observed Bruce Siddle looking a bit tired and worn beyond his years. He is undoubtedly heavier than when he was a patrolman. Somewhat balding and sporting a goatee and glasses, he more closely resembled the image of the doctor or professor rather than a local cop. Siddle carefully explained how "critical incident amnesia" affects police and military in unexpected stressful combat situations. "Fear makes man forget" he pointed out, based upon studies going back thousands of years.

Bruce also told of scientific studies based upon controlled experiments to illustrate memory loss producing "auditory exclusion" like the example I had heard about. Siddle described for the jury an experiment involving a large number of SWAT team officers constantly trained to respond to critical incidents usually involving guns. In a controlled situation each were asked to simulate firing a weapon against a perceived threat. As each officer shot, a staff member stood behind, less than six feet from the participant, and discharged an air pistol with an amplified loud noise. Astonishingly, all but one of the officers said they could not recall hearing the air gun. One female officer claimed to hear birds chirping right outside. When it was checked, a bird's nest on the building suggested she was right, but no one else heard them. A critical incident may distort or disturb auditory or visual observations.

Siddle described an officer interviewed immediately after a shooting could only say the perpetrator had a big gun and belt buckle but could not describe the assailant or incident in any more detail. The perpetrator who was quickly found near the scene had a large shiny belt buckle on his waist near where he held a large .357 Magnum. How does this relate to our case? The focus of that officer was the need to respond to the threat of the weapon, which apparently excluded other sensory impressions. In this case, Siddle pointed out that only the young speeder Josh Wigglesworth claimed to have heard the sound of an automobile horn at the time of the crash. None of the other witnesses heard that noise.

We do not know if an automobile horn made a noise or not, but Siddle explained in a fast moving incident like this one, the mind has a tendency to fill in the gaps in memory when the witness attempts to recreate what happened. Higbee could only have seen the oncoming van and had less than 2.2 seconds to react before the crash, with no prior opportunity to anticipate a collision. Higbee, said Siddle, might well have experienced the "visual narrowing" of all of the senses, which collapse at the stressful event. He explained the phenomenon of "visual tracking" otherwise known as "tunnel vision." Officers are trained not to take their eyes off of the fleeing suspect to make a proper apprehension. Trooper Higbee would have had no idea who the suspect was nor the crime he may have committed at that moment. Therefore, he had to maintain visual tracking and concentrate on his observation of him. Higbee's brief loss of consciousness and his concussion may have contributed to his inability to peer through the darkness of the impact itself in his memory. Just like the officer focused on the perpetrator with the gun, other objects, such as the stop sign in Higbee's peripheral vision may not have been perceived, and therefore not remembered. Yet the officer in each case may try unsuccessfully to recreate in his mind details of what really happened. A mistaken or inaccurate recollection may occur from trying to piece together the incident logically.

Siddle was able to draw upon his own experience to state that Higbee acted, as a reasonable law enforcement officer would have done in all of the circumstances. Higbee did the best he could by slamming on the brakes at the moment he could have seen the fast moving, bright object in his periphery, the Dodge van. He should not be criminally responsible because he did what he was trained to do. He had an instantaneous response, which was fast and appropriate. His failure to see the stop sign at Tuckahoe Road was quite likely a mistake in perception approaching the intersection. Meyer was unable to successfully attack Siddle's expertise or opinion, and by close to 5 p.m. he abandoned any further attempts to cross-examine him. It seemed to me by this time Meyer simply wanted the trial to be over.

We had a brief conversation with the judge after the jury was excused for the day. I wished the judge would agree to provide the jury with a written copy of his instructions on the law, but he declined. I was concerned that the jury really needed to understand what Rob Higbee's state of mind meant when they tried to understand the legal definition of *recklessness*. They would only hear it once from the judge. I hoped the next day would bring an end to this ordeal, but we still had summations and the judge's charge before the jury could deliberate on Rob's fate. My mind raced ahead to closing arguments.

Chapter 13

The trial judge has to explain the law to the jury. The jury's job is to apply the facts that they have found from the evidence they have seen and heard in the courtroom to the law the judge has explained to them. In today's language, it is not only the spin they put on the facts. But how do the lawyers and judge make sure they really understand the elements of the law?

The charge conference takes place outside of the jury's presence. The arguments involve each lawyer trying to convince the judge to include instructions that will benefit his or her client. On Wednesday June 3, 2009, we spent the whole day debating issues while the jury was excused.

I wanted to be sure the jury could hear the definition of "careless driving" which was just a traffic offense, as opposed to the criminal definition of "reckless," which, if found by the jury, could mean Higbee was guilty of a crime. The judge initially rejected my argument, but relented the next day and included it in his final charge. During the conference, I pleaded with the judge not to comment on the perceived inconsistencies he saw in various witnesses' testimony, and in many instances the prosecutor even agreed with me, preferring to be able to make his own remarks during summation. As a result, the judge was persuaded to simply enumerate certain experts who testified, and leave the determination of credibility up to the jury to determine on their own. I felt that was ultimately a fair procedure, because jurors sometimes put too much emphasis on a judge's comments. The jurors needed to interpret the importance of each witness on their own and collectively to reach a decision.

I tried unsuccessfully to have the judge explain that a trooper has a sworn duty to try to apprehend a speeder and obviously he sometimes has to speed himself to catch up with the offender. Instead, the judge left the jury with the thought that they could consider the factor of speed in considering whether the trooper exhibited reckless conduct. I felt that speed and missing the stop sign did not amount to recklessness. I thought the jury might think that was enough to prove criminal wrongdoing unless the judge explained the law more clearly.

The basic problem is that our court rules require the judge to strictly adhere to the Model Jury Charge mandated by our State Supreme Court. In this case, the judge would read the definition as modified by Judge Alvarez's earlier ruling: "A person acts recklessly when he consciously disregards a substantial and unjustifiable risk that death will result from his conduct. The risk must be of such a nature and degree that, considering the nature and purpose of defendant's conduct and the circumstances known to him, disregard of the risk involves a gross deviation from the standard of conduct that a reasonable law enforcement officer would have conducted himself in this situation."

In addition, the judge would charge the state had to prove, beyond a reasonable doubt, that the defendant was aware of and consciously disregarded the risk of death in his operation of the motor vehicle. When these charges were stated in court to the jury, without the benefit of being able to sit and read them over in the jury deliberation room, I was concerned as to whether all of the jurors could understand these explanations. I tried in vain to have the jury hear the lower definition of "negligence" which is the standard used in a civil case seeking money damages. That definition talks about a person who "should be aware of the risk" as opposed to "consciously disregarding the risk" which would make the conduct a crime.

I still felt the jury might be confused if they believed the prosecutor. They might find Higbee guilty if they concluded he should have known where the stop sign was located at the intersection. The prosecutor also reminded the judge that I had told the jury in my opening that the case was important because of the potential loss of personal freedom to my client. He objected to that language, but I reminded the court I used Judge Batten's own words when he introduced the case to the jury. With that, the judge agreed to correctly instruct the jury that sentencing is the exclusive province of the court. I think the jury could figure out that Higbee was facing prison if convicted, even though they might not realize he faced up to twenty years in jail.

Before we left to prepare our closing arguments for the next day, the judge explained the archaic procedure still used in Cape May County to choose the final jury panel of twelve from the forteen then remaining. The clerk would spin the old fashioned wooden wheel with a crank, with all fourteen names rolled into little containers. After the first twelve names were drawn, the remaining two would become alternates, and would sit in a separate room in case something happened to one of the original panel. At least we could be sure this was a fair and random way of choosing the men and women to decide this case. We hoped they would all put aside any preconceived conceptions of this case that they may have absorbed from the media accounts before the trial began. We had to have faith that they would listen to the judge's instructions, and only consider the evidence presented in the court (or the lack of evidence, in my opinion).

* * *

This is my last chance to appeal to common sense. I know in my heart that Rob Higbee is innocent of criminal wrongdoing. A guilty verdict will not only send him to prison...it will have a chilling effect on law enforcement across the country. We train police and first responders and ask them to put their lives on the line for us. Do we want them to second guess themselves and hesitate to do their duty, fearing an honest mistake will send them to jail?

Human imperfection may result in an accident. Deliberate disregard of the law is a crime. How can I make sure the jury understands the difference? The prosecutor, then the judge's charge on the law will follow my summation. The jury will deliberate late today or tomorrow. Now I know what the judge will say to the jury, based upon yesterday's charge conference. I intend to carefully try to use the judge's definitions to ex-

plain them to the jury. Criminal recklessness is a "conscious disregard of a known risk." The civil term negligence implies someone "should have been aware of a risk." Finally, the traffic offense involving careless driving is a "failure to exercise due care and circumspection under the circumstances." I believe the prosecutor will try to confuse the terms and have the jury conclude that Higbee's failure to exactly locate the Tuckahoe Road stop sign in time amounts to reckless, considering the speed he was going.

Remember, Higbee was only semi-familiar with the area and had not stopped anyone there at night before. Is it reasonable to expect him to take note of the backside of a stop sign and remember its exact location in case he suddenly decides to return that way? It was not reckless for Higbee to hover on the brake pedal from the time he saw the stop ahead sign. He was clearly being careful and trying to locate it. "Driver expectation" produced a brief 1.2 seconds of acceleration when he probably saw Wigglesworth's headlights illuminating the stop sign at Roosevelt Boulevard. He made an honest mistake in perception because of the stop sign at Tuckahoe Road, off to the right, is only in his peripheral vision.

When, if ever, did the prosecutor establish the moment Higbee decided to ignore the stop sign and the risk of causing death? Remember Sgt. McMahon's answers to me on cross: "Q. When you consider a 'conscious disregard,' don't you have to be aware of it? In order to stop at a stop sign you have to perceive that stop sign prior to deciding whether to stop or not. Is that so? A. Yes." He concluded the configuration of that "wide throated" intersection was confusing to a motorist. How can "speed" by Higbee be a component of recklessness when his duty calls for apprehending a speeder, but he can't catch him from a complete stop without exceeding the limit himself?

Remember, the Dodge van driven by the seventeen-year old driver was going 42 to 49 miles per hour before impact. At those speeds neither driver would see the other prior to 2.2 seconds before the impact. If Higbee saw the moving white flash of the van, it would seem he acted within one second to slam on his brakes about 150 feet before the crash, but the crash was unavoidable. The prosecution's witness, Ruth, labeled that movement "avoid impact" on his chart. Higbee's reaction was "faster than average." "Significant braking" is how Ruth put it. Sgt. McMahon described it as "heavy braking." All of the state's experts refuted the Taylors' speculation that Higbee "accelerated" into the intersection, disregarding the stop sign.

I knew Meyer would attack Higbee's credibility, so I reminded the jury: "Do you remember Sgt. Ulbrich's testimony? I asked him if Higbee was lying when he thought he had stopped at the stop sign? He answered: 'I don't believe he was deceitful.'" Higbee's rec-ollection was simply inconsistent with the "vehicle dynamics." Both Professor Loftus and Mr. Siddle explained the results of "faulty memory." How can you call his conduct "reckless" when his inten-tion was to stop if and when he saw the stop sign? He simply couldn't see it in time.

What is the other requirement for the prosecutor to prove Hig-bee's conduct was reckless? Where is the gross deviation from the conduct of a "reasonable law enforcement officer"? We produced Lt. Col. Frank Rodgers, who said he would have done the same thing as Higbee. All of the state police witnesses confirmed their policy of not putting on red lights or sirens, when closing the gap. If they put on the red lights or sirens too far away, it might encour-age the violator to flee, among other reasons. So where is the "gross deviation?"

The prosecution produced no witness to establish that element, and we called on experts to deny it. Finally, I thought, I have to focus the jury on Rob Higbee and his state of mind to convince them he is not guilty of a crime.

Turning the prosecutor's opening comments around, I said to the jury: "Bad things happened to very good people in this case." and, "This was an accident, not a crime." Rob Higbee can never erase this tragedy from his mind anymore than can the family of the victims. But he did his duty, exactly as he was trained to do. He had a terrible accident. What changed this from the "A" for Accident on the reports of Sgt. McMahon and Sgt. Ulbrich? They did not change the determination until after they were told of the indictment by the prosecutor's office. Cape May Prosecutor Robert Taylor did not even tell the state investigators about Higbee's indictment until after the case had been presented to the grand jury by his first assistant.

"So how does Prosecutor Meyer convince you of Rob Higbee's criminal state of mind? Use your common sense." I asked: "Why would Trooper Higbee, with all he has to live for, decide to go through a stop sign without stopping? Why would anyone? Have any of you accidentally missed a stop sign ever in your life? Would you want someone to assume it was deliberate and convict you of a crime, instead of careless driving?"

"I respectfully suggest to you that in order for you to conclude that Rob Higbee is guilty of vehicular homicide, you have to conclude that he is 'suicidal' at that moment, because he risks his own life if he goes through the stop sign without looking. Why would he? The state has failed to prove to you, beyond a reasonable doubt, a 'reckless' state of mind necessary to convict Rob Higbee of the crime. We all feel for the victims of this tragedy, but it is an accident, not a crime. We place our fate in your hands." I felt my voice crack with emotion when I turned to look at Rob Higbee and then walked away from the jury.

First Assistant Prosecutor Meyer is the most experienced trial lawyer in the Cape May office. He is meticulous, well organized, and careful. He has designed his presentation to effectively evoke as much sympathy for the victims as he can without injecting reversible error into the trial. If he gets a conviction, an appellate court will carefully scrutinize his closing remarks and he does not want a reversal. I counted on him not to step across the line to attempt to win the case by sheer passion or sympathy for the victims.

As a trained advocate, Meyer immediately responded to my arguments, since he has the last word. We would not be here if Higbee's conduct was "simply negligence," he argued. When things happen, it is different. "Reckless choices may lead to lethal consequences," he intoned. In the context of the charges against Higbee, he paused and looked at the jury and exclaimed: "It's a crime!" Meyer accused the defendant of a "wrongful risk" that "twisted and turned and led to the deaths of Jacqueline and Christine."

He then went through details of all of the exhibits and witnesses in his case. He emphasized the "clearly visible" reflective yellow "Stop Ahead" sign 517 feet before the intersection. Instead of the conclusion that the Roosevelt Boulevard sign was more in the "central vision" of the approaching driver, Meyer argued the converse. He said the Tuckahoe Road stop sign would become "more prominent" at 350 feet away and would have afforded ample time to react, even though the trooper's vehicle was going "almost twice the limit." I really could not object, because the judge would only rule any conclusions are up to the jury to decide.

Meyer's next clever argument was to diffuse my contention that the Tuckahoe Road stop sign was "inappropriately placed," as he put it. He argued it was placed as "close to the curb as it could be" without being in the roadway itself. Of course that is correct. But the curb line was six feet further to the right than one would expect, to provide easy turning to get into the shopping center. Again, misleading, but factually correct. Meyer declared this case was, "not about any contributory defect with the intersection itself," knowing the court's rulings prevented the jury from hearing any detailed discussion of those defects. He said that the placing of the stop sign "a little bit" further to the right is "not that unusual."

"Drivers should be used to widened roadways near strip malls," he added. Meyer showed aerial shots of the scene and routes of travel again. The girls were going west on Tuckahoe Road "without a care in the world." He neglected to point out their exceeding the speed limit. He used the term "driver expectation" to suggest they had no reason to expect a car coming from Stagecoach Road would not yield to them. He also made an argument difficult for me to swallow. This case was, "not about any criminal causation responsibility on the part of the young speeder." Really? Wigglesworth had no legitimate reason to speed. Higbee had a duty to try to apprehend him.

Meyer spoke of the tragic consequences of the defendant Higbee's "reckless" conduct. He then confused the issue by suggesting that somehow Higbee should have immediately "braked and slowed" as soon as he saw the "stop ahead sign." The problem with that logic is there is no uniform distance between "Stop Ahead" signs and stop signs in New Jersey. Higbee would have no way of knowing how far ahead the sign he was seeking was.

Meyer glossed over the impediments to seeing the stop sign at Tuckahoe Road, including the utility poles on the side of the road approaching the sign. He criticized the trooper for "unlimited speed," saying he failed to avoid danger to the public. He then pointed to the "parade of character witnesses," saying he did not suggest Higbee was not a good person. However, there is no exception in the vehicular homicide statute for a "good person."

The prosecutor then neatly avoided the crucial issue as to the lack of proof of a "conscious disregard" of the risk. He stated to the jury: "If we engage in reckless conduct which results in the death of others, then we are responsible for that conduct." That was the conclusion. But, I thought, where is the proof Higbee decided to be reckless? This is not someone who got behind the wheel, knowing he was intoxicated. Meyer warned the jury not to be sympathetic to the defendant because he is a police officer. My mention of his possible loss of liberty was irrelevant and of no concern to the jury. Police do not have "limitless discretion." They can be found guilty "by recklessly pursuing all violators of the law." The "gross deviation" from that of a reasonable law enforcement officer was for not coming to a complete stop at the intersection and looking both ways according to the written NJSP procedures.

Meyer claimed it was not necessary to produce a witness to prove that conclusion; the written standard operating procedure was enough. Ignoring the seatbelt issue, Meyer contended "but for" the defendant's "running the stop sign at the extraordinary speed that he did, they would not have died." He suggested Higbee should have slammed on the brakes three seconds before the impact instead of the last 1.5 seconds. In commenting on Higbee's memory, he implied that if Higbee had made a mistake he would have testified to his misperception, instead of lying about his recollections. He asserted the defendant was "oblivious to his surroundings" and "fixated" on the speeding vehicle ahead. He ran the stop sign, and therefore "no reasonable person" could decide he was not reckless. Prosecutor Meyer concluded: "Justice demands the defendant be held criminally responsible for his reckless behavior," and he told the jury to find Higbee "guilty of two counts of vehicular homicide."

Chapter 14

Judge Batten gave his detailed jury instructions after both summations by the attorneys. The court clerk spun the "ancient wheel" and the two alternates were separated from the final twelve on the jury. All of the jurors stood up as a group and swore upon their oaths to "fairly and impartially render a true verdict in the case between the State of New Jersey and Rob Higbee."

It was almost 4:30 p.m. when the jurors filed out to the Jury Deliberation Room. About fifteen minutes later the judge inquired through the jury administrator if they wanted to continue today. They sent back word, exhausted as they probably were, they wanted to call it a day, and start fresh Friday morning. It would not be fair to do otherwise. The jury was admonished as usual not to read, listen, or talk about the case except when together in the jury room. Judge Batten dismissed them for the night.

Another fitful, sleepless night was ahead for all of us. What did I forget? What more should I have done? I planned for the worst. If Rob was convicted, had I brought out every error on the record at trial to raise on appeal?

I reflected on the positive factors. The judge relented and put in an explanation of the various states of mind in his final charge. He had allowed us individual *voir dire* so we thought we had a fair jury. His use of live court reporters assured us of a complete transcript if we needed it later. I even felt the impact of live TV coverage helped expose this case to public scrutiny and maybe made the jurors even more aware of the importance of this case.

Friday, June 5, 2009. Soon after beginning their deliberations in secret, the jury sent out a note with their first question. They wanted a calculator. Both sides agreed, and the judge complied by sending in a device to the jury room through the court attendant. The debate continued as we waited around the courthouse. Another question followed later in the morning. This time they wanted a ruler. Again, the process repeated, and it was supplied. We waited in and around the court and remained available by cell phone to immediately return if needed. The deliberations continued all day Friday with no verdict. The jury was allowed to go home for the weekend and resume Monday.

The nightmares continued for everyone whose lives had been intertwined for the last two and a half years. I wrestled with concerns about each individual juror now.

Had the ironworker related to split second decision making by my client, involving risk of death or serious injury? Did I paint a clear picture of the scene to the artist? Did the retired nurse understand what the concussion might have done to Rob? Did I provide a logical explanation to the communications worker? Did the physical therapist grasp the human factors? Was the postmaster aware of the intersection? What would the engineer do with the electronic data recording? What would the land surveyor see in the measurements of the aerial photographs? Would the public employment secretary realize police officers are not perfect, that they make mistakes? Would the truck driver relate to the possibility of an accident here, with his hundreds of miles of driving every week? Would the retired naval officer relate to his aircraft carrier experience of perception and reaction time? What about the forelady? Was she as attentive and fair as her body language suggested? Could she be a strong leader in the jury room, calling for the votes when needed?

The jury was excused for the weekend. When they returned Monday morning they asked for a read back of Rob Higbee's testimony. We agreed with the judge's decision that the jury must hear the entire direct and cross, instead of portions they might want to hear. That was to take all day, with the monotone reading of the notes by each court reporter from the witness stand. I tried to assure Rob I thought this was a good sign. Higbee's words were there, but his gaze to the family and his sincere expression to the jury were not present by the reading of the words alone. I hoped the jury would picture his honest and forthright appearance as his testimony was repeated again. Would they relate to the "gentle giant" and his careful devotion to duty? Or would they think he lied to cover up some "reckless attitude?"

The session continued all morning. The jury was provided lunch by the court in their deliberation room away from any outside influences. We left the courthouse to wait on the second floor of the nearby Bellevue Restaurant, an old converted State Police Barracks. Our entire trial team of Burgos, Vitale, Ridgeway, Rob, his wife Beth, and my wife Petie, gathered together for the wait. Many supportive troopers, friends, and relatives of Rob joined us in the room. We had been upstairs away from the public where we met every day for lunch during the long trial. But this day was different.

Everything we could do was done. Sometimes the STFA chaplain had been with us. He could not be there this day. So I took it upon myself to help Rob in one more way. I asked our entire group to hold hands in the middle of the room. We recited the *Lord's Prayer* together. I added my personal prayer that the jury would find the truth. I also prayed that verdict would be soon.

We returned to the courtroom after the break and the read back of the Higbee testimony lasted until close to 4:40 p.m. The jury was sent out again to continue deliberations. The judge said he was going to call them back shortly to see if they wanted to adjourn for the day. I requested that he let the jury continue for a while to let them make the decision on their own. We waited. About 4:45 p.m. on June 8, 2009, we were all startled when the jury sent word they wished to return. As reported in the media, the packed courtroom was silent before the verdict was announced. I am told that my client's face was flushed and mine was ashen. Judge Batten asked the forelady if they had reached a verdict. "Yes, your Honor," and it was unanimous on each count. Finally, the best two words we could ever hear were repeated twice, by the forelady, for each count of the indictment: "*Not Guilty.*"

My client and the troopers remained stoic and concealed their emotions. However, I admit I somewhat lost my composure as I stepped into the well of the court as the jurors started to leave. Amidst some anguished tears I exclaimed: "Thank God! And thanks to the jury!" as the court was adjourned.

At her request, Rob Higbee met privately with the victim's mother, Maria Caiafa, in the small court anteroom. Their conversation will remain private. My client and I spoke briefly with the media gathered outside the courthouse. At last the long ordeal of the trial was finally over.

* * *

In our society, the mere accusation of wrongdoing may be enough to destroy a person's reputation forever, even if the defendant is eventually exonerated. The *right to trial by jury* remains the bulwark of our criminal justice system of the United States of America, along with the the common sense of twelve good citizens chosen to sustain it.

Chapter 15: 2012

Trooper Rob Higbee returned to full duties with the New Jersey state police. He was promoted to Detective 1, and currently does not have assignments involving patrol duties. He and his wife Beth continue to raise two young daughters.

Maria Caiafa and her family continue to try to cope with their tragic loss.

Chris Burgos was elected president of the New Jersey State Troopers Fraternal Association after the retirement of Davy Jones.

I am still in private practice of law, as is Donna Lee Vitale, although neither of us is associated with a law firm.

Manny Ridgeway is still a private investigator.

Judge Batten still presides in superior court in Cape May County.

First Assistant Prosecutor J. David Meyer and Chief of County Detectives Eugene Taylor have retired.

Robert Taylor still holds his post as county prosecutor.

The twelve courageous and conscientious citizens who served on the jury in the Higbee trial have returned to their normal lives.

There are many more individuals who will never forget the jury's contribution to our system of justice.

Trial Notes:
What the Jury Didn't See

The jury did NOT have the following information to use in its deliberations during the trial:

• None of the "artist renderings" of the accident from the perspective of Trooper Higbee (*see pages 143-145*) produced by the defense.

• No photographic representations and descriptions produced by the defense, detailing improvements made to the intersection by the county (*see page 150*) after the accident. This includes the old 30" diameter stop sign on northbound Stagecoach Rd. that was obscured by utility poles that was replaced only three months afterwards with a 48" stop sign with two reflector poles; a new red and yellow blinking light that was installed in the intersection; and improved street lighting to focus directly on the new stop sign at Tuckahoe Road

• Reports of 26 accidents at this same intersection, which prompted the local government to urge the county, in two seperate resolutions, to install a traffic control device. The decision to install such a device had instead been deferred, in anticipation that the cost could be borne by a new shopping center developer.

• Prosecutor Taylor withheld from the public the prosecution's knowledge of the speeder being chased by Trooper Higbee, until it was disclosed at the trial itself.

• The grand jury saw no reports, photographs, or documentation, and heard from only one witness from the prosecutor's staff, who overstated the speed of Higbee's vehicle prior to the accident.

- This case was the *first* ever that a New Jersey superior court judge admitted a Ford electronic data recorder (EDR) to be considered in a criminal jury trial.

- The state's EDR expert Richard Ruth had previously consulted with the defense, but because he had not been immediately retained, he contacted the county prosecutor, requesting to become a paid expert testifying on the prosecution's behalf.

- The state's own accident reconstruction expert, Sgt. John McMahon, stated in his report to the prosecutor that the stop sign at Tuckahoe Road was further to the right than "normal" for a driver going north on Tuckahoe Road, and that it posed a problem for perception at night

- The prosecutor sought and received another independent accident reconstruction expert report, but did not produce the expert at trial because it confirmed Sgt. McMahon's findings.

- Throughout the State of New Jersey there were 179 fatal accidents at stop sign intersections in the four years preceding this accident, but no driver had ever been indicted for vehicular homicide without evidence of some impairment or deliberate action on the part of the driver.

- Trooper Rob Higbee was the *first* law enforcement officer to ever be indicted under these circumstances in the State of New Jersey.

Diagrams
PowerPoint
Photographs
Newspaper Clippings

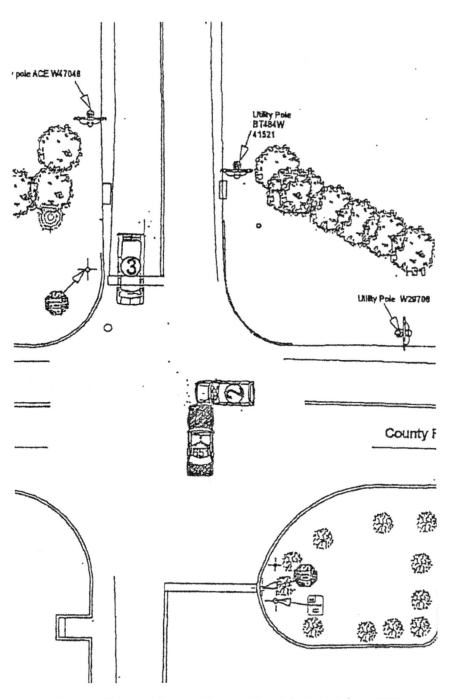

Diagram #1 of crash scene by Det. Sgt. John McMahon, NJSP

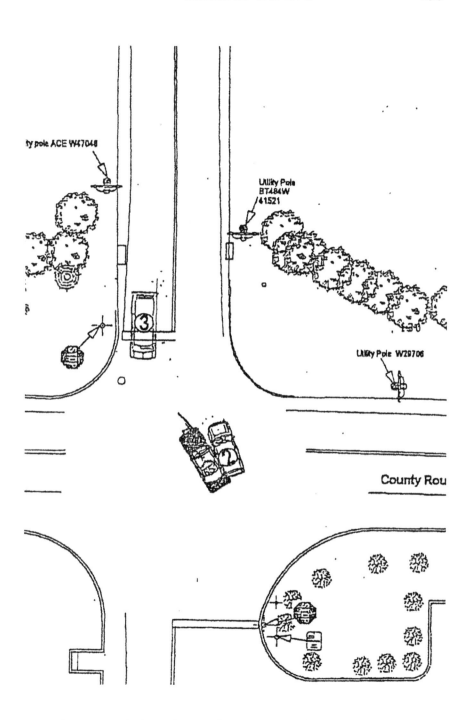

ty pole ACE W47048

Utility Pole
BT484W
/41521

Utility Pole W29706

County Rou

Diagram #2 of crash scene by Det. Sgt. John McMahon, NJSP

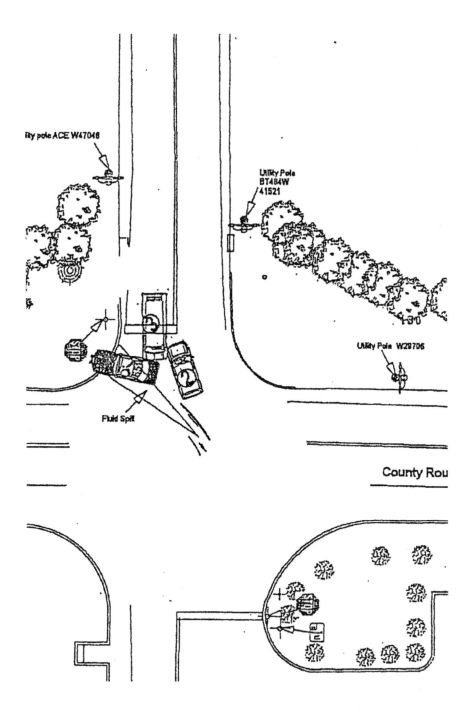

Diagram #3 of crash scene by Det. Sgt. John McMahon, NJSP

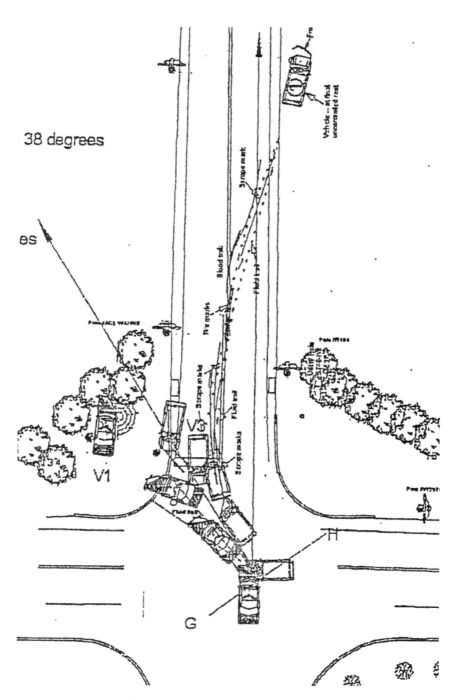

Diagram #4 of crash scene by Det. Sgt. John McMahon, NJSP

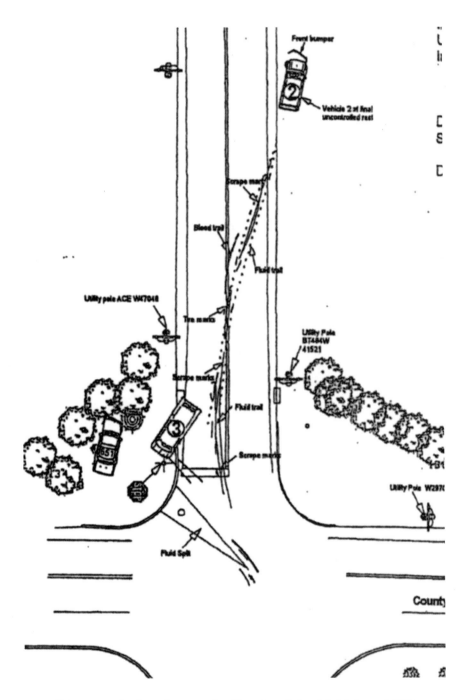

Diagram #5 of crash scene by Det. Sgt. John McMahon, NJSP

The following is a portion of the defense's
opening arguments PowerPoint presentation.

The Accident Scene

- Marmora, Upper Township, NJ
- Intersection of Stagecoach and Tuckahoe
- Approximately 10:00 PM, Sept. 27, 2006.
- A dark and poorly marked intersection with a very wide, paved shoulder and a stop sign further to the right than normal.

Trooper Robert Higbee

- A New Jersey law enforcement officer *on duty,* performing his *sworn* obligation at the time of the incident.
- Attempting to "close the gap" and apprehend a speeder.

New Jersey Policy

According to N.J. Attorney General policy, a trooper shall "close the gap" between his patrol vehicle and a speeder's vehicle *before* activating his emergency lights and siren.

The Collision

- Trooper Higbee was closing the gap northbound on Stagecoach Road.
- A Dodge van was traveling westbound on Tuckahoe Road.
- Resulted in a tragic *accident* — it was not a *crime.*

Criminal Charges

- This is a *criminal* trial, <u>not</u> a *civil* trial.
- Trooper Higbee is charged by the Cape May County prosecutor with "vehicular homicide" — a *criminal* act.

Definitions

- <u>Vehicular Homicide</u> is defined as *recklessly* causing the death of another with a vehicle.
- A person acts *recklessly* when he *consciously disregards* the substantial and unjustifiable risk that death or serious bodily injury will result from his conduct.

To Consciously Disregard

- One must be *aware* of something's existence before deciding to *consciously disregard* it.
- In this case, the prosecution must prove the trooper was aware of the risk, before they can conclude he *consciously* disregarded it.
- In other words the prosecutor must prove the trooper *ignored* the risk.

Elements of Vehicular Homicide

To establish guilt, the prosecutor must prove beyond a reasonable doubt all three elements:

- That the defendant was driving a vehicle
- That the defendant caused the death of a person or persons
- That the defendant caused that death by driving *recklessly*.

The Stop Sign At Tuckahoe Road

· The Prosecutor must prove Trooper Higbee was aware of the stop sign's existence and its location an that he *consciously disregarded* the stop sign at Tuckahoe Road.

· In order to sustain his burden of proof in this case, the prosecutor must show a *gross* deviation from the standard of conduct of a *reasonable law enforcement officer*.

Presumption of Innocence

· The Burden of Proof is always on the Prosecution.

· The defendant is always entitled to the presumption of innocence throughout the trial.

(l) Higbee's view approaching Tuckahoe Road intersection
(r) Speeder's headlights on Roosevelt Blvd. stop sign
Artist Rendering by Carl L. Rosner, Margate NJ

CLOSING THE GAP

Higbee's view from patrol car approaching Tuckahoe Rd. intersection.
Artist Rendering by Carl L. Rosner, Margate NJ

Higbee's view just prior to collision.
Artist Rendering by Carl L. Rosner, Margate NJ

Higbee and victim's mom meet in courtroom.
Courtesy Press Of Atlantic City

Robert Higbee at counsel table during the trial.
Courtesy *In Session*

State Trooper Higbee vehicular homicide trial

Crime or accident?

Opening arguments shed different light on 'explosive event'

State Police Trooper Robert Higbee, center, stands with his attorney, D. William Subin, right, as the jury enters the courtroom Wednesday.

Higbee

(Continued from A1)

nearby Wawa convenience store for the next day's breakfast.

What happened next, Meyer said, was "an explosive event" as Higbee's car crashed into

C. BECKER

J. BECKER

difficult to see at best.

Subin said that Higbee also

Courtesy *Press Of Atlantic City*

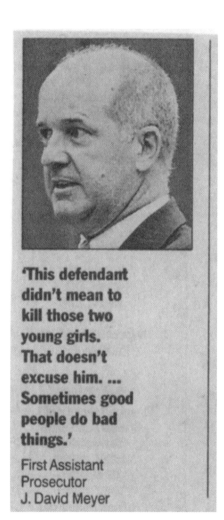

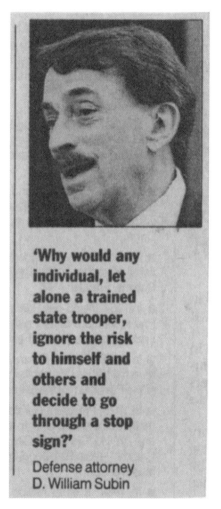

'This defendant didn't mean to kill those two young girls. That doesn't excuse him. ... Sometimes good people do bad things.'

First Assistant Prosecutor J. David Meyer

'Why would any individual, let alone a trained state trooper, ignore the risk to himself and others and decide to go through a stop sign?'

Defense attorney D. William Subin

Courtesy *Press Of Atlantic City*

Crash intersection *after* improvements by the county.
Photos courtesy Liske Forensics, Inc. Identification by Carl L.Rosner

Higbee and Subin listen to Prosecutor Meyer's closing argument.
Courtesy *In Session*

"Not Guilty"

Staff photo by Dale Gerhard

Robert Higbee, right, shows relief as he and defense attorney D. William Subin hear the verdict.

Robert Higbee (r), defense counsel Bill Subin (c),
and Investigator Manny Ridgeway (l) listen as the jury
returns a verdict of "Not Guilty.". Courtesy *Press of Atlamtic City*